Flowers to the Rescue

The Healing Vision of Dr. Edward Bach

by Gregory Vlamis

HEALING ARTS PRESS
ROCHESTER, VERMONT

Healing Arts Press
One Park Street
Rochester, Vermont 05767

Library of Congress Cataloging-in-Publication Data

Vlamis, Gregory.
Flowers to the rescue:
the healing vision of Dr. Edward Bach / by Gregory Vlamis.
p. cm.
Bibliography: p.
Includes indexes.

ISBN 0-89281-286-9 (pbk.)

1. Flowers — Therapeutic use.
2. Flowers — Therapeutic use — Case studies.
I. Title
RX615.F55V55 1988
615'.321 — dc19   88-23533
CIP

Printed and bound in the United States

10   9   8   7   6   5   4   3

Healing Arts Press is a division of Inner Traditions International, Ltd.

Distributed to the book trade in the United States by Harper and Row Publishers, In
Distributed to the book trade in Canada by Book Center, Inc., Montreal, Quebec
Distributed to the health food trade in Canada by Alive Books, Toronto and Vancou

Flowers to the Rescue

About *Rescue Remedy*, a unique natural stress
reduction formula made from English wildflowers,
developed by Dr. Edward Bach in the early 1930s.
Contains new material and photographs hitherto
unpublished.

NOTE TO THE READER

Neither the author nor the publisher of this book make any claims as to the medicinal effectiveness of the Bach Flower Rescue Remedy. The material presented in this work represents a compilation of information, which was researched by the author both in the United States and Great Britain.

The author is not a physician and is not able to reply to any correspondence or questions about the use of the Rescue Remedy. However, if you know of additional sources of information, or have used the Rescue Remedy and wish to share your experiences for possible inclusion in future editions of this book, contact Gregory Vlamis, P.O. Box A3237, Chicago, Illinois 60690, U.S.A.

'Gregory Vlamis has made a fine contribution to the understanding of the Bach Flower Remedies and one which will greatly increase our awareness of these wonderful healing agents. His account of their development by Edward Bach, supplemented by very practical descriptions of their use, forms a valuable treatise for which we are grateful.' — *Maesimund Panos, MD, DHt, former President, National Center for Homeopathy, Washington, D.C.; co-author of 'Homeopathic Medicine at Home' (Tarcher).*

'I am glad that Gregory Vlamis has taken the trouble to collect all these testimonies to the Bach Flower Remedies. Medical research into them is long overdue.' — *Alec Forbes, MA, DM, FRCP, formerly member Expert Advisory Panel on Traditional Medicine, World Health Organization; medical director Bristol Cancer Help Centre, and author of 'The Bristol Diet: a Get Well and Stay Well Eating Plan' (Century).*

'An outstanding reference work, *Flowers to the Rescue* is both a reference tool and reader for all those interested in the Bach Flower Remedies and especially Dr. Bach's combination formula Rescue Remedy. Mr. Vlamis has excelled in bringing together numerous case studies on the current use of Rescue Remedy, many by top physicians in the field. Additionally, the inclusion of two out-of-print philosophical works by Dr. Edward Bach makes this book a *must* for all those interested in whole person healing.' — *Leslie J. Kaslof, author of 'Wholistic Dimensions in Healing' (Doubleday) and President of the Dr. Edward Bach Healing Society, North America.*

'. . . a valuable record of how Dr. Bach's work has continued in the 50 years since his death. It is a well organized book of impressive and thorough research.' — *Julian Barnard, author of 'A Guide to the Bach Flower Remedies' (C. W. Daniel).*

'*Flowers to the Rescue* shows us the impressive range of experience from health professionals and consumers with the Bach Flower Remedies. This book provides strong testimony to the value of these flower remedies and encourages us all to use them for the various trials and tribulations of modern life.' — *Dana Ullman, MPH, co-author of 'Everybody's Guide to Homeopathic Medicines' (Tarcher), and Director of Homeopathic Educational Services, Berkeley, California.*

'This book will be of great interest to many veterinarians. The wonderful accounts of the efficacy of Rescue Remedy in animals is particularly fascinating'. — *Richard H. Pitcairn, DVM, PhD, author of 'Dr. Pitcairn's Complete Guide to Natural Health for Dogs and Cats' (Rodale Press).*

DEDICATION

To those who suffer and are in distress; to Dr. Edward Bach, and to his spirit; to the Bach Centre for carrying on his good work; to my daughter, Roxanne Vlamis; to my father, Constantine Vlamis, and especially to my mother, Roxanne Vlamis Santos—for her tremendous caring and support.

Contents

Contents

Acknowledgements

A great many people helped to put this book together. I am especially indebted to:

Nickie Murray and John Ramsell, current curators of the Dr. Edward Bach Centre, for their co-operation, general support and permission to use case studies from their files, and the right to reproduce *Ye Suffer From Yourselves* and *Free Thyself* by Dr. Edward Bach.

Leslie Kaslof for his wisdom, advice, encouragement, and pioneering of the Bach Flower Remedies in North America.

Ralph Kaslof for his commitment to the work.

Mary Hayden, Dr. Bach's sister and Evelyn Varney, his daughter, for sharing their memories and photographs.

Dr. Charles K. Elliott for his kind comments and foreword.

Dr. J. Herbert Fill for the introduction.

Andrewjohn and Eleni Clarke for their hospitality in the United Kingdom.

Deborah Mills for her meticulous typing.

I wish to deeply thank the many who responded to my letters and questionnaires, as well as those hundreds of people throughout the world who provided case studies, kind words and encouragement for the completion of this work.

The following, whom I warmly thank, have contributed in one way or another:

Anne Catherine, Didier and Georgette Basilios, Mark Blumenthal, Michael Bookbinder, Bruce Borland, Thomas Boyce, Mary Carter, Robert and Sharon Corr, Marsha DeMunnik, Sonny Delmonico, Leonard and Nilda Durany, Ron Eager, Gloria Early, Marilyn Preston Evans, Professor Norman R. Farnsworth, Marie Firestone, Demos Fotopoulos, Dr. Benjamin G. Girlando, Fred Hahn, Yvonne Hillman, Judy Howard, Celia Hunting, Jeanne Janssen, Margie Kuyper, Stewart Lawson, Dr. Robert Leichtman,

Acknowledgements

Sanna Longdeń, Linda Nardi, Robert Krell, Nancy Madsen, Marilyn Marcus, Dick and Rita Marsh, Molly Morgan, Malcolm Murray, Beverly Oldroyd, Ann Parker, Dr. Richard Pitcairn, Katherine Prezas, Victoria Pryor, Melanie Reinhart, Mary Rita, John-Roger, the Royal London Homoeopathic Hospital, London, England, Vera Rugg, George Santos, Sue Smith, Mrs. Spalding, Robert Stevens, Serita Stevens, the University College Hospital Medical School, London, England, Ginny Weissman, Bette, Eileen and Francis Wheeler, Ingrid Williams, and Jennifer Wright.

A special thank you to Bonnie Corso, Elinore Detiger, Faye Waisbrot Honor, Jack Honor, Bobbie Philip, and Lisa Sperling.

Most of all an exceptional acknowledgement to Sharon Steffensen for being the inspiration for this work.

Preface

During the past fifty years, many prominent medical doctors, homoeopaths,[1] and other health care professionals have reported the successful treatment of adult patients, children, and animals with the thirty-eight flower remedies discovered by the late Dr. Edward Bach.

Prepared from the flowers of wild plants, bushes, and trees, the Bach Flower Remedies do not directly treat physical disease, but help stabilize the emotional and psychological stresses reflecting the root cause. The stress factors include such things as fear, loneliness, worry, jealousy, and insecurity. Carried to the extreme, these emotions lower the body's natural resistance to disease. By assisting the integration of emotional, psychological, and physiological patterns, the remedies produce a soothing, calming effect, thereby allowing the body to heal itself.

These flower remedies are simple to use, and relatively inexpensive; moreover, they have reportedly been shown to be consistently effective when chosen correctly.

All thirty-eight of the Bach Flower Remedies have been included in the *Supplement to the Eighth Edition of the Homoeopathic Pharmacopeia of the United States*[2], and are officially recognized as homoeopathic drugs. This was primarily due to the efforts of Leslie J. Kaslof, author, researcher, and pioneer in the field of holistic health.

---

1. For editorial consistency the traditional spelling "homoeopathy" has been used wherever the word appears except when "homeopathy" (a more contemporary spelling) is used in a book's title.

2. Official compendium of homoeopathic drugs.

Most widely known of all the Bach remedies is the Rescue Remedy, a combination of five of the Bach flowers. Rescue Remedy is the emergency first aid remedy. It is extremely useful in many situations and generally works very quickly.

I first observed the effects of Rescue Remedy on a friend who was grieving over his father's death. So dramatic was his relief that I felt compelled to explore Bach's discoveries in more depth. Eventually, this led me on a four-month journey through the United Kingdom, where I came upon rare photographs, unpublished writings and letters of Dr. Bach's, all kindly supplied to me by his relatives and close friends.

I have been most impressed by the consistent reports of success in the use of Rescue Remedy, both in simple and complicated circumstances. These reports justify further investigation and controlled studies.

Though Rescue Remedy is called for in diverse circumstances, it is not a panacea or a replacement for orthodox medical care. It is used during minor stressful periods to develop emotional and psychological equilibrium, and during crisis situations, to ease emotional and psychological stress before and during emergency medical treatment. Many medical doctors, homoeopaths, other physicians and health care professionals throughout the world, carry the Rescue Remedy in their emergency kits or on their person for use in such circumstances.

The case studies contained in this book are authentic and based on extensive research and personal interviews. They illustrate, however, only a small part of the Rescue Remedy's versatility.

If only a few people obtain relief from their suffering and distress through the use of the Rescue Remedy, the purpose of this work will have been accomplished.

Gregory Vlamis
Chicago, Illinois
25 January 1986

Foreword

Dr. Edward Bach's (1886-1936) contribution to medicine—his system and philosophy known as the Bach Flower Remedies—provides us with an ideal of health beyond the absence of symptoms. True well-being comes from within. Like Hippocrates, Paracelsus, and Hahnemann, Bach knew that good health depended on spiritual, mental, and emotional factors being in harmony.

The effects of disharmony are shown by negative moods and thoughts that assail each of us at times. Bach understood that these, in turn, can affect the body, depleting it of strength and vitality by blocking the life force necessary to our existence at all levels. True healing—restoring harmony—opens up the channel for this vital flow of life.

Dr. Bach astutely noted that illness is ultimately beneficial and constitutes a period of true refinement and purification.

Heal Thyself, Bach's brilliant essay, published by C. W. Daniel, 1931, should be mandatory for every student of health. In it Bach states: "There is a factor which science is unable to explain on physical grounds, and that is why some people become affected by disease whilst others escape, although both classes may be open to the same possibility of infection. Materialism forgets that there is a factor above the physical plane which in the ordinary course of life protects or renders susceptible any particular individual with regard to disease, of whatever nature it may be."

Devoted and inspired research, coupled with Bach's unique background as a physician, pathologist, immunologist, and bacteriologist, led him to create one of the most comprehensive state-of-the-art systems of healing known, a gentle, simple system that works and is available to all.

The Bach Flower Remedies can be used with orthodox or complementary, alternative systems of medicine. Nature's wisdom is always added to any treatment employed. In ancient wisdom, medicine existed in closest communion with spiritual vision. Today, Dr. Edward Bach's holistic system embodies this ancient ideal.

Current scientific research is proving that a person's mental and emotional state can influence, positively or negatively, ills ranging from the common cold to cancer.

This new field of research, psychoneuroimmunology, is rapidly gaining the respect of the medical establishment. Mental states and emotions are now seriously considered in the total treatment of most illness.

I hope that progressive scientists examine the varied merits of the Bach Flower Remedies. Bach's philosophy of health offers us inner peace, harmony, and hope for the future.

Charles K. Elliott, MB, BCh,
MFHom, MRCGP, MLCO, AFOM RCP,
London; Former Physician to
Her Majesty Queen Elizabeth II;
co-editor of *Classical Homoeopathy* (Beaconsfield,
England: Beaconsfield Publishers Ltd., 1986)

Introduction

I have been using the Bach Flower Remedies in my practice for over ten years and have found them, including the Rescue Remedy, invaluable when used correctly. I use them almost exclusively instead of tranquilizers and psychotropics, and in many cases they alleviate the problem when all else has failed. The Bach Flower Remedies are extremely sophisticated in their alleviation of specific moods, gentle and yet potent in balancing the body's subtle energy fields. Though subtle in their action, the Bach Flower Remedies are not placebos.

The Bach Flower Rescue Remedy deserves its special place in the Bach literature. Its action is unique, as the reader will discover in the subsequent pages. Until this present work, little has been made available on this subject.

In writing this book, Gregory Vlamis has produced a well-written summary for the professional as well as the general public. The reader is given practical information on how to use the Bach Flower Rescue Remedy in dealing with the crises of everyday life, from acute to chronic. *Flowers to the Rescue: The Healing Vision of Dr. Edward Bach* is easily readable and abundantly filled with case accounts, illustrating the great variety of applications of this amazing gift of nature. As a psychiatrist, I distinctly appreciate the preventive value of the Bach Flower Remedies and Rescue Remedy as a powerful and safe alternative to tranquilizers without their characteristic side effects.

It is my sincere wish that all, especially my colleagues and medical students, become aware of the Bach Flower Rescue Remedy and Bach's work in order to experience the remedy's efficacy and to confirm the insights of a modern medical genius.

With many people now losing faith in modern medicine, this is the right era for us to learn about this time-honored method of healing that uses preparations obtained from English wildflowers.

Thanks to the author, we have been given a valuable opportunity to become aware of a most precious adjunct to medicine. This book and the Bach Flower Rescue Remedy should be in every health care professional's armamentarium, in every home, vehicle, and first aid kit.

J. Herbert Fill, MD, psychiatrist;
former New York City Commissioner
of Mental Health; author of
The Mental Breakdown of a Nation
(New York: Franklin Watts, 1974)

PART I

"Everyone of us is a healer, because every one of us at heart has a love for something, for our fellow-man, for animals, for nature, for beauty in some form. And we every one of us wish to protect and help it to increase. Everyone of us also has sympathy with those in distress, and naturally so because we have all been in distress ourselves at some time in our lives.

"We are all healers, and with love and sympathy in our natures we are also able to help anyone who really desires health. Seek for the outstanding mental conflict in the patient, give him the remedy that will assist him to overcome that particular fault, and all the encouragement and hope you can, and then the healing virtue within him will of itself do all the rest."

Dr. Edward Bach

Dr. Edward Bach: Healing Pioneer

The spirit of Edward Bach lives in the lush green country-side of England—in the trees, plants, and flowers he used for his remedies.

Born on September 24, 1886, at Moseley, outside Birmingham, he was the eldest of three children.

Independent in outlook, even from his earliest years, Bach had a great sense of humor, which sustained him through many trials. As a child, he loved to meditate, and he often roamed the countryside alone, pausing just to sit and to contemplate the beauty of nature. As he grew, his love for nature and life developed into a great compassion for all living things, especially those in pain or distress. His overwhelming desire to help the suffering compelled him to become a physician.

Even before he began his medical studies, Bach observed that standard medical treatment was often more palliative than curative. He became convinced that there had to exist a simpler method of healing, one that could be applied to all diseases, including those regarded as chronic or incurable. He decided that he would search out those long-forgotten truths of the healing arts.

To accomplish this he sought medical training. In 1912, Bach obtained the Conjoint Diploma of MRCS, LRCP, and in 1913 he received his MB and BS[1] degrees from the Univer-

---

1. MRCS—Member Royal College of Surgeons; LRCP—Licentiate of the Royal College of Physicians; MB—Bachelor of Medicine; BS—Bachelor of Surgery.

Dr. Edward Bach, 1921. (Courtesy E. Varney)

sity College Hospital Medical School, London. In 1914, he received the Diploma of Public Health from Cambridge.

Though occasionally referred to as batch; his family, close friends and colleagues called him bache as in the letter H, meaning little one, petite, or dear. Today, most people, unaware of this specific pronunciation, commonly pronounce Bach as they would the name of the well-known musical composer.

In the early years of his practice, Bach became a respected pathologist, immunologist, and bacteriologist. Still, he was never satisfied with the results of orthodox medical treatment. Bach observed that although pills, drugs, and surgery were helpful in relieving specific symptoms, they did little to fight long-term and chronic disease. At this time, Bach set out to find and develop a treatment for the relief of chronic illness. In 1915 he accepted a position at University College Hospital as assistant bacteriologist. There he discovered that certain strains of intestinal bacteria had a specific relationship to the cause of chronic disorders. He began preparing vaccines from these bacteria. The results of his research exceeded all expectations.

Complaints such as arthritis and severe headaches were alleviated, and patients began to report remarkable improvements in their general health.

Pleased with these results but not with the side effects of vaccination, Bach searched for a method of treatment that would be gentle yet effective.

In 1919, after taking a position at London Homoeopathic Hospital, he discovered the works of Dr. Samuel Hahnemann, the founder of homoeopathy.[2] Bach found much of Hahnemann's philosophy similar to his own. It was similar to the same principles and philosophy which had inspired him from the beginning of his medical career. Hahnemann's concept—"treat the patient and not the disease"—was to become the basis of Bach's system of healing, a system he was to discover many years later.

Bach began preparing his bacterial vaccines homoeopathically and administered them orally. These oral vaccines, or nosodes, as they are called, seemed to fulfill all his

2. A system based on the theory and practice that disease is cured by remedies which produce in a healthy person effects similar to symptoms in the patient. The remedies are normally administered in minute or even infinitesimal doses, thus minimizing the potential for toxic side effects often found with the use of most allopathic drugs.

expectations. Hundreds of chronic cases were treated, yielding exceptional results.

Welcomed enthusiastically by the medical profession, these vaccines became widely used, and they are still used today by homoeopaths and medical doctors in England, America, and Germany. Bach's works on intestinal toxemia appeared in the *Proceedings of the Royal Society of Medicine*,[3] 1919-1920, and in 1920-1921 additional works appeared in the *British Homoeopathic Journal*.[4] During his career, Bach contributed many other original articles to the British medical and homoeopathic journals. Of particular acclaim was his book *Chronic Disease: A Working Hypothesis* (London: H.K. Lewis & Co., Ltd., 1925), co-authored with Dr. C.W. Wheeler, his highly respected homoeopathic colleague.

Despite these successes, Bach was still not satisfied. He felt that by treating only physical disorders, he was overlooking the real issues of health and the cure of disease.

Disease, he concluded, was the result of disharmony between a person's physical and mental state; illness, the physical manifestation of negative states of mind. Bach noted that deep disharmony within the sufferer, such as worry, anxiety, and impatience, so depleted the individual's vitality that the body lost its natural resistance and became vulnerable to infection and other illnesses. Though Bach came to this understanding in his own right, it had been propounded in the past by such noted individuals as Hippocrates, Maimonides, and Paracelsus, and more recently substantiated by the research of Drs. Hans Selye, O. Carl Simonton, and many others working in the field of stress-related disorders. In light of the tranquillity and inner har-

---

3. "The Nature of Serum Antitrypsin and Its Relation to Autolysis and the Formation of Toxins," and "The Relation of the Autotryptic Titre of Blood to Bacteria Infection and Anaphylaxis," Teale, F.H. and Bach, E. *Proc. of the Royal Society of Medicine*, (13) December 2, 1919, pp. 5, 43, respectively.

4. "The Relation of Vaccine Therapy to Homoeopathy," and "A Clinical Comparison Between the Actions of Vaccines and Homoeopathic Remedies," *British Homoeopathic Journal*, 10:2 April 1920 p. 6, 11:1 January 1921 p. 21, respectively.

mony Bach always experienced when out in nature, he felt that the solution to disease-causing states was to be found among the plants, trees, and herbs of the field.

Obeying his intuition, which had proved successful in his earlier experiments, Bach decided to visit Wales in 1928.

There, by a mountain stream, he gathered the flowers of Impatiens (*Impatiens glandulifera*) and Mimulus (*Mimulus guttatus*). Later that year, he discovered the wild Clematis (*Clematis vitalba*). Preparations of these flowers were later administered to his patients, producing immediate and noteworthy results.

At this time, Dr. Edward Bach was at the height of his medical career. But in 1930, again following his inner conviction, Bach courageously closed his laboratory, left his London home, and spent his remaining years traveling throughout Wales and Southern England, perfecting his new system of medicine. Walking hundreds of miles in his search for curative plants, he discovered thirty-eight remedies—all, with one exception, derived from flowering plants and trees he found in the English countryside.

As his work progressed, he realized that his own senses were becoming more refined. For several days before he found a remedy, he would intensely experience the physical and mental symptoms of the disease that this remedy was to cure. Then he would go into the fields and find the appropriate healing flower. He could place a petal or flower in his palm or on his tongue and experience the effects of the plant on his mind and body. Coupled with extensive research and application, the newly found remedies proved extremely successful.

Bach immediately published his discoveries in the leading homoeopathic journals of the day. It was also his intention that this new system be made available to the lay person as well as to the professional community. Bach described his system of medicine in inexpensive booklets, the first three entitled *Heal Thyself, Free Thyself,* and the *Twelve Healers.* (See page 159 for references.)

Dr. F.J. Wheeler, a close friend and colleague, verified

Bach's findings by using many of the flower remedies in his own practice. He gave Bach valuable feedback and encouraged him to continue his research.

Bach treated many patients, particularly during the winter months, with his new remedies and his unique system of diagnosis. He developed a special love for the people of Cromer (Norfolk, East Anglia, England), where he settled and took up practice, feeling especially close to the fishermen and lifeboat men. What Bach most admired about these men was their 'down-to-earth' lives. Not caring for money, Bach often received gifts of fish, eggs, or vegetables in payment for his medical services.

It was at Cromer, during a terrible storm, that Bach first used three of the flowers found in the Rescue Remedy to aid an ailing crew member of a ship wrecked in the storm. Unconscious, foaming at the mouth, and almost frozen, the

The Bach Centre, Mount Vernon. (Courtesy Here's Health)

man seemed beyond hope. At repeated intervals, Dr. Bach moistened the patient's lips with the remedies as the unconscious fisherman was being carried up the beach to a nearby house. Within minutes, the patient regained consciousness.

Bach continued with his work in this small community until 1934 when, at Sotwell near Wallingford, Oxfordshire, England, he located a small house named Mount Vernon. Here he was to spend the final two years of his life.

Bach's humanity, as much as his genius, drew people to him. Believing that anyone who needed help or sought it for others should be given the tools for healing, he advertised his remedies in local newspapers. As a result, in 1936 the General Medical Council threatened to remove him from its register. In his reply, Dr. Bach wrote, "I consider it the duty and privilege of any physician to teach the sick and others how to help themselves....My advertisements were for the public good, which, I take it, is the work of our profession." Reconsidering its charge, the General Medical Council never did remove Dr. Bach's name from its register, and to this day Bach's work has been a major source of inspiration to doctors and the general public worldwide.

For further information on Dr. Bach's life, the reader is encouraged to consult *The Medical Discoveries of Edward Bach, Physician*, by Nora Weeks (London: C.W. Daniel, 1940), published in the United States by Keats, New Canaan, Connecticut, 1979.

The Work of Bach Continues

Following Dr. Bach's passing in 1936, Victor Bullen and Nora Weeks carried on his work at Mount Vernon. Nora, who during her years as trustee of the Bach Centre at Mount Vernon wrote *The Medical Discoveries of Edward Bach, Physician* was, along with Victor Bullen, mainly responsible for the growth of Bach's work until their respective deaths in 1978 and 1975.

Victor Bullen and Nora Weeks worked with Dr. Bach, carrying on his work at Mount Vernon, after Bach's passing in 1936. (Courtesy Bach Centre)

Nickie Murray and John Ramsell worked together at the Bach Centre with Nora Weeks, till her passing in 1978. From that time to the present they carried on Bach's work, and are the current curators of the Bach Centre. (Courtesy Bach Centre)

In the early 1960s, Nickie Murray and then her brother, John Ramsell, joined the Bach Centre, and after Nora's and Victor's passing continued on as trustees with the same devotion and commitment as their predecessors.

During their walks about the country, Bach had taught Victor and Nora the names of every wildflower and every tree, saying, "You must recognize them by the leaves of their seedlings so that you can know them and make friends with them from their very beginning."

To this day, the Bach Flower Remedies are prepared exactly as Dr. Bach had done, taken from Bach's original wildflower locations. In addition to preparing the Bach remedies and overseeing appointed distributors in many parts of the world, the Dr. Edward Bach Centre answers inquiries from around the world and publishes *The Bach Remedy News Letter.*

Mount Vernon will always be the center of Dr. Bach's work. Before Bach departed, he made it a point to emphasize: "Though the work will ever increase, keep your life and the little house as it is, for simplicity is the keyword to this system of healing."

Dr. Edward Bach, c.1931-32. (Courtesy Bach Centre)

The Philosophy of Bach on Health and Disease

For many years, since he had come upon the works of Samuel Hahnemann, Bach had concentrated on "treating the patient, not the disease." His personal philosophy on health and disease was an important element in his discovery and development of the flower remedies.

Bach himself was deeply religious, believing all mankind was created in a state of perpetual Unity with God. Man's Soul—the real Self—is most directly connected to the Creator and ever leads man to a higher good. Although the physical body is temporary, the soul is everlasting. Moreover, the soul infuses and guides the personality, comprising the mind and the body as a whole.

Dr. Bach also believed that each person has a mission in life. He wrote:

"...this divine mission means no sacrifice, no retiring from the world, no rejecting of the joys and beauty of nature; on the contrary, it means a fuller and greater enjoyment of all things; it means doing the work we love to do with all our heart and soul whether it be housekeeping, farming, painting, acting or serving our fellow-man in shops or houses. This work, whatever it may be, if we love it above all else, is the definite command of our soul."

Taking this idea a step further, Bach defined health as perfect harmony between the soul, mind, and body. Disease, then, results from a lack of harmony between these elements.

When we do not follow the dictates of our soul by following our intuition—our knowledge of "good"—disease develops in our body as a result of our resistance. This resistance occurs, "when we allow others to interfere with our purpose in life, and implant in our minds doubt, or fear, or indifference." Emotions such as fear and anger, as well as cruelty and rigidity of thought, surface when we are diverted from the soul's purpose, and, consequently, from the personality's true development.

But disease, according to Bach, is paradoxically a healing process because it warns us against carrying our wrong actions too far. Once disease has manifested itself, we must modify our erring mental state and bring it back into line with the convictions of our soul, if we are to be healed. When this realignment begins, so does the physical healing; and both will continue until mind and soul are again in tune and the body is well.

Thus, Bach argued that disease is not an evil, but a blessing in disguise whose purpose is "solely and purely corrective." Indeed, the area where we have physical difficulties is a mirror of our mental difficulties. Bach wrote:

"If you suffer from stiffness of joint or limb, you can be equally certain that there is stiffness in your mind; that you are rigidly holding on to some idea...which you should not have. If you suffer from asthma, you are in someway stifling another personality; or from lack of courage to do right, smothering yourself....The body will reflect the true cause of disease such as fear, indecision, doubt—in the disarrangement of its systems and tissues."

Complete healing Bach said, depended on four factors:

• The realization of the Divinity within us, and our consequent knowledge that we have the ability to overcome all harm.

• The knowledge that disease is due to disharmony between our personality and our soul.

• Our desire and ability to discover the fault that is causing the conflict.

• The removal of that fault by our developing the opposing virtue.

Over and over again, Bach emphasized that if we want to return to health, we must expect change. Disease was not to be conquered by direct fighting, since "darkness is removed by light, not by greater darkness." To help us make the necessary changes in our personalities, he urged that we learn to replace our weaknesses with strengths, such as substituting acceptance for intolerance.

Bach realized, of course, that "certain maladies may be caused by direct physical means, such as those associated with some poisons, accidents, and injuries, and gross excesses; but disease in general is due to some basic error in our constitution—the conflict of personality and soul..."we have so long blamed the germ, the weather, the food we eat as the causes of disease; but many of us are immune in an influenza epidemic; many love the exhilaration of a cold wind and many can eat cheese and drink black coffee late at night with no ill effects. Nothing in nature can hurt us when we are happy and in harmony."

Believing that physical disease manifested as a result of negative mental and emotional states, Bach opposed those aspects of modern medicine that directed efforts only toward the healing of the physical. He felt that drugs were often counter-productive because the temporary relief they produced in many instances suggested a complete return to health while negative mental and emotional patterns continued unchecked. True healing was postponed, and the inevitable result was more serious illness later on.

When Bach developed his flower remedies, his aim was to effect a healing on a much deeper level than just the physical. Bach, referring to the remedies once wrote:

"they are able...to raise our very natures, and bring us nearer to our Souls....They cure, not by attacking disease, but by flooding our bodies with the beautiful vibrations of our Higher Nature in the presence of which disease melts as snow in the sunshine."

As a physician, Bach believed that doctors should play the part of adviser and counselor to a patient, providing guidance and insight. The patient must come to realize that he has responsibility for his own healing. He must be prepared to face the truth that his illness was caused by faults that lie within himself, and he must have the desire to rid himself of those faults.

One of the unique advantages of the Bach Flower Remedies is that they can be applied before the first signs of physical illness, thereby preventing disease before it takes hold in the body. Bach noted that "before almost all [serious] complaints there is usually a time of not being quite fit, or a bit run down; that is the time to treat our conditions, get fit and stop things going further." Even a temporary state of conflict between the personality and soul may render the body susceptible to infectious agents that are ready to attack when the body's normal defenses are weak.

A more in-depth explanation on Dr. Bach's Philosophy can be found in *Heal Thyself*, by Edward Bach (London: C.W. Daniel, 1931), and in *The Bach Flower Remedies*, by Drs. Edward Bach and F.J. Wheeler (New Canaan, Connecticut: Keats, 1977). Previously unavailable philosophical writings, *Ye Suffer From Yourselves* and *Free Thyself* are included in appendices A & B.

The Thirty-eight Bach Flower Remedies

The following chapter provides an overview of the various conditions and situations to which all thirty-eight of the Bach Flower Remedies apply.

Additional information on the use of the entire thirty-eight remedies, may also be found, either in *The Twelve Healers and Other Remedies,* by Edward Bach (London: C.W. Daniel, 1933) or in *The Bach Flower Remedies* (New Canaan, Connecticut: Keats, 1977).

Since 1936, the thirty-eight flower remedies discovered by Dr. Bach have been used to restore emotional and psychological equilibrium to individuals during periods of both mild and intense stress. Within his system, Bach classified the following seven major emotional and psychological states:

- **FEAR**
- **UNCERTAINTY**
- **INSUFFICIENT INTEREST IN PRESENT CIRCUMSTANCES**
- **LONELINESS**
- **OVERSENSITIVE TO INFLUENCES AND IDEAS**
- **DESPONDENCY OR DESPAIR**
- **OVERCARE FOR THE WELFARE OF OTHERS.**

Within every classification, he described their variations.

The following is a brief summary of all the thirty-eight Bach Flower Remedies and their uses. These are listed within their appropriate categories. This list is not intended as a definitive explanation of all the Bach remedies and their uses. For further information consult the references listed above.

1. FEAR

*Rock Rose (*Helianthemum nummularium*) for extreme terror, panic, hysteria, fright, and nightmares.

*Mimulus (*Mimulus guttatus*) for known fears; for example, fear of heights, pain, darkness, poverty, death, being alone, of other people, etc. Also for timidity and shyness.

Cherry Plum (*Prunus cerasifera*) for fear of losing mental and physical control; inclination to uncontrollable rages and impulses, with fear of causing harm to oneself or others, for example suicidal tendencies,** or losing one's temper.

Aspen (*Populus tremula*) for vague fears and anxieties of unknown origin, a sense of foreboding, apprehension, or impending disaster.

Red Chestnut (*Aesculus carnea*) for excessive fear or over-concern for others—especially loved ones, for example; overconcern during their illness, automobile trips, etc., always anticipating that something unfortunate may happen to them.

2. UNCERTAINTY

*Cerato (*Ceratostigma willmottianum*) for those who doubt their own ability to judge and make decisions. They are constantly seeking others advice and are often misguided.

---

*One of the original twelve healers.

**The Bach Flower Remedies and Rescue Remedy are not meant to take the place of emergency medical treatment. In all cases requiring psychiatric or medical attention, a licensed physician should be called immediately.

*Scleranthus (*Scleranthus annuus*) for those who are indecisive, being unable to decide between two choices, first one seeming right then the other. They may also be subject to energy or mood swings.

*Gentian (*Gentianella amarella*) for those easily discouraged, in whom even small delays may cause hesitation, despondency and self-doubt.

Gorse (*Ulex europaeus*) for feelings of despair, hopelessness, and futility.

Hornbeam (*Carpinus betulus*) for that Monday-morning feeling of not being able to face the day; for tiredness and a tendency towards procrastination; for those who feel that some part of their bodies or minds need strengthening.

Wild Oat (*Bromus ramosus*) for those dissatisfied in their current career or life style, their difficulty however, is in determining exactly what career to follow.

3. INSUFFICIENT INTEREST IN PRESENT CIRCUMSTANCES

*Clematis (*Clematis vitalba*) for those who tend toward escapism living more in the future than in the present; for lack of concentration, daydreaming, lack of interest in present circumstances, and spaciness.

Honeysuckle (*Lonicera caprifolium*) for those dwelling too much in the past, reminiscing about the "good old days;" nostalgia, and homesickness.

Wild Rose (*Rosa canina*) for those who are apathetic and have resigned themselves to their circumstances, making little effort to improve things or to find joy.

Olive (*Olea europaea*) for total mental and physical exhaustion and weariness; for sapped vitality from a long illness or personal ordeal.

White Chestnut (*Aesculus hippocastanum*) for persistent, unwanted thoughts, mental arguments, or preoccupation with some worry or episode.

Mustard (*Sinapis arvensis*) for deep gloom that comes on for no apparent reason, bringing sudden melancholy and heavy sadness.

Chestnut Bud (*Aesculus hippocastanum*) for those who fail to learn from experience, continually repeating the same patterns and mistakes.

4. LONELINESS

*Water Violet** (*Hottonia palustris*) for those whose preference is to be alone; seemingly aloof, proud, reserved, self-reliant, sometimes 'superior' in attitude. Capable and reliable they will advise, but not get 'personally' involved in others affairs.

*Impatiens** (*Impatiens glandulifera*) for those quick in thought and action but often impatient, especially with those who are slower than they; for those who show irritability through lack of patience.

Heather (*Calluna vulgaris*) for those talkative persons who constantly seek the companionship of anyone who will listen to their troubles. They are self-absorbed, generally poor listeners, and have difficulty being alone for any length of time.

5. OVERSENSITIVITY TO INFLUENCES AND IDEAS

*Agrimony** (*Agrimonia eupatoria*) for those not wishing to burden others with their troubles, covering up their suffering with a cheerful facade; they often seek escape from pain and worry through the use of drugs or alcohol.

*Centaury** (*Centaurium umbellatum*) for those who have difficulty in saying no, often becoming subservient in their desire to serve others; anxious to please they can be easily exploited, neglecting their own interests.

Walnut (*Juglans regia*) for stabilizing emotions during periods of transition, such as teething, puberty, adolescence, and menopause; for breaking past links and adjusting to new beginnings, such as new jobs, adjusting to new residence, cultures, or even relationships.

Holly (*Ilex aquifolium*) for negative feelings such as envy, jealousy, suspicion, revenge, and hatred; for all states showing a need for more love.

6. DESPONDENCY OR DESPAIR

Larch (*Larix decidua*) for those who, despite being capable, lack self-confidence. Anticipating failure, they often do not make a real effort to succeed.

Pine (*Pinus sylvestris*) for those not satisfied with their own efforts, who are self-reproachful and suffer much from guilt and the faults they attach to themselves, feeling they should or could have done better. They are often quick to blame themselves for the mistakes of others.

Elm (*Ulmus procera*) for those who over extend themselves and become overwhelmed and burdened by their responsibilities.

Sweet Chestnut (*Castanea sativa*) for those who feel they have reached the limits of their endurance; for dark despair, when the anguish seems to be unbearable.

Star of Bethlehem (*Ornithogalum umbellatum*) for mental and emotional stress during and following such traumatic experiences as grief, loss and accidents.

Willow (*Salix vitellina*) for those who have suffered from some misfortune or circumstance they feel was unjust or unfair. As a result, they become resentful and bitter toward others.

Oak (*Quercus robur*) for those who despite illness and adversity never give up. They are brave and determined to overcome all obstacles in order to reach their intended goal.

Crab Apple (*Malus pumila*) for feelings of shame, uncleanliness, or fear of contamination; for poor self-image, particularly as it relates to parts of or growths on the body. Will assist in detoxification and the cleansing of wounds, both internal and external.

7. OVERCARE FOR WELFARE OF OTHERS

*__Chicory__ (*Cichorium intybus*) for those who are overfull of care and possessive of those close to them; they can be demanding and self-pitying, with a need for others to conform to their ideals.

*__Vervain__ (*Verbena officinalis*) for those who have strong opinions, always teaching and philosophizing. They are easily incensed by injustices, and when taken to the extreme can be overenthusiastic, argumentative, and overbearing.

Vine (*Vitis vinifera*) for those who are strong-willed leaders in their own right. However, when carried to extremes, they can become autocratic, dictatorial, ruthless, and dominating.

Beech (*Fagus sylvatica*) for those who, while desiring perfection, easily find fault with people and things. Critical and intolerant at times, they may fail to see the good within others, overreacting to small annoyances or other people's idiosyncrasies.

Rock Water (*Aqua petra*) for those who are strict and rigid with themselves in their daily living. They are hard masters to themselves, struggling toward some ideal or to set an example for others. This would include strict adherence to a life style or to religious, personal, or social disciplines.

PART II

The cure of the part should not be attempted without treatment of the whole. No attempt should be made to cure the body without the soul, and, if the head and the body are to be healthy, you must begin by curing the mind.... For this is the great error of our day in the treatment of the human body, that physicians first separate the soul from the body.

Plato (427-347 B.C.) *Charmides*

Rescue Remedy:
Bach's Emergency Medicine

R escue Remedy was named by Dr. Bach for its calming and stabilizing effect on the emotions during a crisis.

The following chapter describes the composition of Rescue Remedy, its historical origin, its scope of application, and use.

Rescue Remedy is made up of the following five Bach Flower Remedies.

*Impatiens (*Impatiens glandulifera*) for the impatience, irritability, and agitation often accompanying stress. This may sometimes result in muscle tension and pain.

*Clematis (*Clematis vitalba*) for unconsciousness, spaciness, faintness, and out-of-the-body sensations, which often accompany trauma.

*Rock Rose (*Helianthemum nummularium*) for terror, panic, hysteria, and great fear.

Cherry Plum (*Prunus cerasifera*) for fear of losing mental or physical control.

Star of Bethlehem (*Ornithogalum umbellatum*) for trauma, both mental and physical.

Dr. Bach first used three (Rock Rose, Clematis and Impatiens) of the five ingredients in the Rescue Remedy with two men shipwrecked in a gale off the beach at Cromer on

---

*One of the original twelve healers.

the Norfolk coast of England, where Bach did much of his work. The men had lashed themselves to the mast of their wrecked barge and survived for five hours in a howling gale before a lifeboat could reach them. The younger man was almost frozen, delirious, and foaming at the mouth. Dr. Bach ran into the water, meeting the rescuers, and began to apply these remedies to the man's lips. Even before the sailor could be stripped of his wet clothes and wrapped in a blanket, his relief became apparent as he sat up and began conversing. After a few days of hospital rest, he had recovered completely. Bach later combined the remedies Cherry Plum and Star of Bethlehem, for their particular virtues, to the first three remedies, thereby completing the formula we know today as the Rescue Remedy.

Using the Rescue Remedy

Rescue Remedy is available in both liquid concentrate and cream form. It can be used alone or in combination with any other of the Bach Flower Remedies. In addition, it has been deemed effective when used with other remedial agents and various therapeutic modalities such as chiropractic, dentistry, and massage. As reported in the case studies, Rescue Remedy has been shown to be non-toxic, non-habit-forming, and free from side effects. However, it should be noted that **Rescue Remedy is not meant to be a panacea or a substitute for emergency medical treatment.** In serious situations such as accidents, a doctor or ambulance should be called immediately. Many times during emergencies, however, before qualified medical assistance can arrive, the sufferer may experience a variety of emotional and psychological disturbances. These can include fear, panic, severe mental stress, and tension. Rescue Remedy used during this critical period, has been reported to significantly assist in stabilizing the victim emotionally until help arrives.

Additionally, Rescue Remedy is reported to have a positive calming and stabilizing effect in a broad range of stressful situations including nervousness, anxiety, and the stress arising from bereavement, great fright, hysteria, anguish, and desperation.

Even minor incidents that cause stress, such as arguments, exams, speeches, and job interviews, are made easier with Rescue Remedy.

Application

1. Place four drops of Rescue Remedy concentrate into a quarter glass of liquid.

2. Sip every three to five minutes or as often as necessary. Hold in mouth a moment before swallowing.

If water or other beverages are not available:

1. Rescue Remedy may be taken directly from the concentrate bottle (dilute if alcohol-sensitive) by placing four drops under the tongue. Drops may also be added to a spoonful of water if desired.

2. Hold liquid in mouth a moment before swallowing.

For those unable to drink:

• Rub the remedy directly from the concentrate bottle on the lips, behind the ears, or on the wrists.

NOTE: Rescue Remedy, as with all Bach Flower Remedies, assists in restoring emotional balance. Once balance is achieved, the need for and the effect of the remedy diminishes. Therefore, no discernible effect will be noticed if a person takes Rescue Remedy when he is not distressed.

External Use

Rescue Remedy cream is prepared in a neutral, homoeopathic, non-allergenic and non-abrasive cream base. It has been reported extremely effective when applied to bruises, bumps, sprains, scratches, hemorrhoids, minor burns, insect bites, and minor inflammations. It has also been reported useful in healing minor cuts when applied directly. Using the liquid Rescue Remedy orally, in conjunction with Rescue Remedy cream, will help ease emotional upset associated with any of the above conditions. **If Rescue Remedy cream is unavailable the liquid may also be applied externally with equal effectiveness, especially for painful blows, minor burns, sprains, etc.** In addition, the cream rubbed on is said to be effective in reducing acute muscle stiffness. To use:

• Apply by smoothing gently into the affected area, or by applying on a piece of gauze to wounds or abrasions. Use as often as required, continuing applications for a short time even after the condition has improved.

Veterinary Use

Mix four drops of Rescue Remedy in an animal's drinking water or food. In the case of large animals such as cows and horses, ten drops to a bucket of water have been reported to be greatly beneficial in those conditions calling for the use of Rescue Remedy. Examples include accidents, pre- and postsurgical conditions, and birthings. If an animal is traumatized or unconscious, Rescue Remedy may be used directly from the concentrate bottle or diluted in a small glass of water and rubbed on and in the mouth or beak, behind the ears, or on other soft points of the body.

Plant Use

Researchers, such as Cleve Backster, as reported in the book *The Secret Life of Plants*, by Peter Tompkins and Christopher Bird (New York: Harper & Row, 1973), have shown plants to be affected by environmental stimuli, as well as interrelations between them and other forms of life. It comes as no surprise, then, that the Rescue Remedy has also been used to ease trauma in transplanted botanicals, drooping flowers, and injured trees. Ten drops in a watering can or sprayer, applied regularly for a day or two, will help reduce the very real shock that plants can experience and help revitalize them. In the vegetable garden, the addition of five to ten drops in the water at planting time or at any other point in the growing season has been reported of benefit to crops.

Case Studies: Professional and Consumer Use

The following case studies have been meticulously compiled and researched by the author over a three-year period. Because of the highly personal and sensitive nature of these accounts, measures were taken to protect the privacy of individual contributors using the Rescue Remedy at home. This was accomplished by listing only their city, state, or country in place of personal names. Additionally, personal consumer reports were edited when necessary, for grammatical consistency and clarity; still remaining true to the intent and experience originally described. Subsequently, quotation marks have not been included in any of the personal consumer case reports.

Wherever cases involving the professional use of Rescue Remedy appear, names of the contributing doctors or health care professionals are included, along with the names of their cities, states, or countries reported to us at the time.

All professional testimonies and case studies appear here with the full knowledge and written consent of the contributing doctors and health practitioners. Except for minor grammatical changes, indicated by editors brackets[ ] these testimonies and case studies appear verbatim.

All case studies included in this book were obtained through personal interviews, questionnaires, and letters from contributors in the United States and abroad. In addition, the Bach Centre's newsletter files were consulted and used.

NOTE: Rescue Remedy is not meant to take the place of emergency medical treatment. In all instances requiring proper medical attention, a competent physician should be notified at once.

Cases where only the name of a country was available, were primarily extracted from published Bach Centre newsletters.

It should be noted that while many of the case studies included here are impressive, they are meant only to serve as a reference—not to sensationalize or make unfounded claims of efficacy for the Rescue Remedy.

From the hundreds of reports available, every effort was made to present the reader a balanced representation of cases. Though great attention was paid to categorizing these case studies, some overlapping occurs.

Professional Testimonies

The following is a compilation of professional reports on the use of Rescue Remedy both in the United States and abroad. Highly valued, Rescue Remedy is clearly an important healing tool, used by physicians as well as by many other health care professionals worldwide.

All testimonies, as well as professional case studies and consumer reports appear in arbitrary order in their respective sections and categories.

Professional use and reports on Rescue Remedy are prolific; though seeming extensive, the statements presented here represent only a fraction of its overall use.

Physicians practicing in the United Kingdom often have numerous titles and credentials; wherever these references appear in the text, the style of the British Medical Journal was followed, whereby only the two highest medical degrees are listed. While there are many medical doctors (MD's) practicing in the United Kingdom, many British physicians have distinguishing credentials other than MD. Ninety-eight percent of the British testimonials and case studies included in this book were written by practicing physicians of one degree or another. Since all professional credentials are abbreviated, the following glossary has been included to clarify their meaning.

AFOM	—Associate Faculty Occupational Medicine (UK)
BAc	—Bachelor of Acupuncture (UK)
BAO	—Bachelor of the Art of Obstetrics (UK)
BCh	—Bachelor of Surgery (UK)
BChir	—Bachelor of Surgery (UK)
BS	—Bachelor of Surgery (UK)
BVetMed	—Bachelor of Veterinary Medicine (UK)
CA	—Certified Acupuncturist (USA)
ChB	—Bachelor of Surgery (UK)
DC	—Doctor of Chiropractic (USA & UK)
DCH	—Diploma in Child Health (UK)
DDS	—Doctor of Dental Surgery (USA & UK)
DM	—Doctor of Medicine (same as MD) (UK)
DN	—Doctor of Naprapathy (USA)
DPH	—Diploma in Public Health (UK)
DO	—Doctor of Osteopathy (Different Lic.Requirements in USA & UK)
DObst RCOG	—Diploma Royal College Obstetricians and Gynaecologists (UK)
DVM	—Doctor of Veterinary Medicine (USA)
DVSM	—Doctor of Veterinary Surgery and Medicine (UK)
FRCP	—Fellow Royal College of Physicians (UK)
LRCP	—Licentiate Royal College of Physicians (UK)
LRCS	—Licentiate Royal College of Surgeons (UK)
MB	—Bachelor of Medicine (UK)
MD	—Medical Doctor (USA & UK)
MFHom	—Member Faculty of Homoeopathy (UK)
MLCO	—Member London College of Osteopathy (UK)
MRCP	—Member Royal College of Physicians (UK)
MRCGP	—Member Royal College of General Practitioners (UK)
MRCS	—Member Royal College of Surgeons (UK)
MRCVS	—Member Royal College of Veterinary Surgeons (UK)
ND	—Naturopathic Doctor (USA & UK)
PhD	—Doctor of Philosophy (USA & UK)
(UK)	—United Kingdom
(USA)	—United States of America

"As a healer I choose to use only those systems of healing that prove themselves to be effective in my work. It is well known by all people of knowledge that disease begins on a much deeper level than the physical. This, great men have taught for thousands of years. One such man in our time was the English physician and scientist Dr. Edward Bach, who not only taught this truth but became a great herbalist, discovering those special plants and healing waters which work on this deepest of levels. His system is respected and known as the Bach Flower Remedies.

"I have used these Bach remedies and the combination Rescue Remedy for over eight years and have found them to be gentle but powerful healing medicines. Emotional upsets ranging from the deepest fear to pride and jealousy are gently resolved within and scattered like the dust in a wind. We would not want to be without the Rescue Remedy for emergencies. Hysteria and grief, or the trauma resulting from accidents, are quickly stabilized by the oral administration of Rescue Remedy and, when required, the topical use of the cream. It will even soothe the minor upsets of the child who is crying and irritable.

"Though there are many healing tools for good, Dr. Bach's combination, Rescue Remedy, is one of the finest for emergencies and trauma. I strongly encourage all people, those who have pets and range animals, and especially those with children, to keep the Rescue Remedy at home or on their person, for emergencies happen when they are least expected."

Sun Bear, medicine chief,
Bear Tribe, Spokane, Washington

"I use the Bach remedies extensively in my practice. They have proven very helpful with patients wishing to clarify issues in their minds, develop their potential, and see the positive qualities within themselves.

"Rescue Remedy is very useful in calming children who are having temper tantrums, and it alleviates their apprehension when they have to get shots. I also use it with good results for the fears and anxieties that patients experience in my office.

"I keep Rescue Remedy in my car, in my house, and in every room of my office. I even take it myself when I have a hard schedule."

G.S. Khalsa, MD,
Lathrup Village, Michigan

"The Bach Flower Remedies are underused in practice and are long overdue to be researched. I have found them extremely useful in a large number of cases. I would use Rescue Remedy without hesitation in any acute situation in addition to any other appropriate measure indicated by the circumstance."

Julian Kenyon, MD, director,
Center for Alternative Therapies,
Southampton, England

"In my experiences at the Old London Homoeopathic Hospital, now the Royal London Homoeopathic Hospital, I have found Rescue Remedy and the Bach Flower Remedy, Star of Bethlehem to be of great value."

Margery G. Blackie, MD,
former Physician to
Her Majesty Queen Elizabeth II;
author of *The Patient: Not the Cure*
(London: Macdonald & Janes, 1979;
also published in the USA by
Woodbridge Press, 1978)

"In my practice, I treat the whole person but specialize in skin and allergic diseases. I have seen many older, despondent patients sit around and scratch themselves almost raw. With kindness, patience, and the use of the Bach remedies, especially Rescue Remedy, many of these people have been remarkably helped without the use of lotions and drugs."

James Q. Gant Jr., MD,
Washington, D.C.

"I always carry Rescue Remedy in my purse. You never know when an emergency may arise and you will need it."

Maesimund Panos, MD,
Tipp City, Ohio;
former president, National Center for
Homeopathy, Washington, D.C.;
co-author of *Homeopathic Medicine at Home*
(Los Angeles, California: Tarcher, 1981)

"I have used the Bach Flower Remedies for over thirty years and have found them, especially the Rescue Remedy, to be of great value in my practice. I recommend that everybody carry the Rescue Remedy, as one never knows when it may be needed in an emergency. Dr. Bach made a great contribution to the world; he was indeed an absolute medical genius. The Bach Flower Remedies are a missing key to the new medicine of the future."

Aubrey Westlake, MB, BChir,
Fordingbridge, Hampshire, England;
president of The Psionic Medicine Society;
author of *The Pattern of Health*
(London: Shambhala Press, 1961)

"The Rescue Remedy is a very useful first aid remedy when used for acute crises, anxieties, and fears. I have often been surprised at the good results it has achieved when other measures have failed. I consider the Bach Flower Remedies a major contribution to medicine."

Robin G. Gibson, FRCP, DCH,
consultant physician to the
Glasgow Homoeopathic Hospital,
Glasgow, Scotland

"I have used the Rescue Remedy for myself and my family, as I prefer this type of 'trial' prior to deciding if a treatment is appropriate for my professional use. I have found Rescue Remedy extremely effective in relieving a wide variety of acute emotional stresses. I have also found the Rescue Remedy cream equally valuable when applied topically to bruises, bumps, sprains, swellings, etc."

Richard E. Behymer, MD,
Camptonville, California

"I would like to say how marvelous the Rescue Remedy is, both in cream and liquid form. I always carry them both with me. It never ceases to amaze me how well they work. I recommend it to many of my patients and am always hearing of its good results."

Nicola M. Hall, principal,
The Bayly School of Reflexology,
Worcester, England

"I have had amazing results, both with the individual Bach Flower Remedies and especially with Rescue Remedy. I've seen the Rescue Remedy used on people who have had accidents as well as other traumatic experiences. It works almost instantly to calm them down, and when either the Rescue Remedy liquid or cream is applied directly on the affected area, it quickly reduces any swelling or trauma there."

Eugene C. Watkins, ND,
Southfield, Michigan

"I find the Bach Flower Remedies very effective in treating anxiety, depression, mental upsets, and emotional problems. I use them in combination with other homoeopathic medicines and dietary modifications when called for, especially in cases of hyperactivity in children."

S.J.L. Mount, MB, MRCP,
former consultant to the
Royal London Homoeopathic Hospital,
London, England; medical consultant to the
London Natural Health Clinic, London, England;
author of *The Food and Health of Western Man*
(New York: John Wiley and Son, 1971)

"In my practice I often use a technique that treats imbalances of the temporal mandibular joint in the jaw. With most people, there is usually tremendous emotional tension stored in this area, and during treatment a patient may bring emotions to a conscious level. One dose of Rescue Remedy usually has an immediate and profound calming effect on them."

Gerald Brady, DC,
St. Paul, Minnesota

"I use the Rescue Remedy frequently, particularly for acute wounds such as cuts, bruises, swellings, etc. It works almost immediately to calm the system and take away nausea, faintness, or hysteria. It is also very useful during acute asthma attacks. The remedy quiets the patient almost immediately. I have also used it for morning sickness in pregnant women and in many cases of animal injury, especially with birds that fly into glass doors or windows. However, it should not be counted on as the only means of treatment, but as an aid to remove panic and trauma, giving the physician time to prepare for more specific procedures."

James E. Williams, CA,
DelMar, California

"I use quite a lot of Rescue Remedy for myself and my patients. Anyone who uses it while under pressure and stress will find that it works far better than any tranquillizer."

Elizabeth Ogden, LRCPI, LRCSI,
Dublin, Ireland

"In my experience I have seen positive results from the use of the Bach Flower Remedies, including Rescue Remedy, and feel that they definitely merit further investigation."

Jonathan Shore, MD,
Mill Valley, California

"We use a great deal of Rescue Remedy, both the liquid and cream, and find that the liquid, taken internally, helps to reduce emotional upsets, while the cream hastens the healing of conditions ranging from cuts to scalds; we also massage the cream into painful joints to alleviate discomfort. We find all the Bach remedies, especially the Rescue Remedy, to be invaluable in our work here, and would not want to be without them."

Beryl James, physical therapist,
The Roy Morris Clinic,
Oswestry and Wigan, England

"I am a volunteer in a local hospice program [a place where terminally ill people can go to spend their last days, without the use of life-support systems], and Rescue Remedy really comes in handy for the families I deal with. I give it to people who are going through emotional or physical difficulties, and it always makes them feel better."

B.J.D.,
San Antonio, Texas

"I use the Bach Flower Remedies quite extensively in my practice. Most patients tell me that within the first few days of taking the remedies they feel a greater sense of emotional balance. I find the Rescue Remedy as useful with my own family as with my patients. Any time there is a trauma, it will often calm a person down to the point where nothing else is needed. Rescue Remedy liquid is also extremely useful in dealing with grief, emotional upset, or when one is nervous or off-center.

"I have also used the Rescue Remedy cream for sprains, muscle strains, bruises, bumps, and minor burns and find it to be remarkably effective in reducing the pain, swelling, and inflammation of these conditions. I recommend that Rescue Remedy be in everyone's first aid kit. It's easy to use, inexpensive and produces no toxic side effects."

Kirby Hotchner, DO,
Des Moines, Iowa

"The most useful treatment for trauma that I know is Dr. Bach's Rescue Remedy. It is [an] invaluable first aid (along with proper medical treatment) for the victims of accidents, [and for] injuries [and] fright—especially in children—or [in] sudden bad news. The liquid comes in a handy little dropper bottle which [practically] lives in my bag. I also keep a bottle in my car [for similar situations]."

Barbara Griggs, London, England;
author of *The Home Herbal: A Handbook
of Simple Remedies* (London: Pan, 1983;
originally published by Jill Norman &
Hobhouse, Ltd., 1982); and *Green
Pharmacy: A History of Herbal Medicine*
(London: Jill Norman & Hobhouse Ltd., 1981;
also published by Viking Press, New York, 1981)

"I recommend that Rescue Remedy be kept on hand especially during childbirth, both for the mother and those attending. I have found it extremely valuable for relieving tension in a crisis. Rescue Remedy is an absolute must, used in childbirth, especially if there's a long labour or if forceps are used. In addition, Rescue Remedy can also be used for the newborn to assist with the trauma of the birth experience. It can be rubbed on the wrists, temples, scalp, or navel area."

Lorraine Taylor, BAc,
Oxford, England

"I use the Rescue Remedy as an alternative to prescribing Valium. It sometimes proves to be of invaluable assistance."

D. McGavin, MRCGP, DCH,
Maidstone, Kent, England

"Of the various remedies and techniques used in this office, none are more valued and respected than the Bach remedies."

Nicholas Ashfield, DC,
Toronto, Canada

45

"I find the Rescue Remedy very useful in calming and assisting patients, particularly during the transitional effects of strong treatment procedures. We often use Rescue Remedy during extensive cranial work and in other mechanical adjustments.

"I feel that Rescue Remedy helps to minimize the physiological, mental, and emotional stress that often accompanies manipulative procedures. It is an important adjunct for the doctor as well as facilitating the patient's healing response."

Joseph Unger Jr., DC,
St. Louis, Missouri

"I use Rescue Remedy with elderly patients who live alone; it seems to assist them in handling their lives more effectively. When these patients face a task they must struggle with, Rescue Remedy calms and stabilizes them quite effectively. I recommend Rescue Remedy for use in the later years and to calm and stabilize in all forms of stress."

Hilda Saenz de Deas, BAc,
Oxford, England

"I have used the Bach Flower Remedies in my clinical practice for over twenty-five years and have had very good results, especially in conjunction with other modalities. In raising my own family of four boys, my wife and I found that certain remedies were very helpful indeed."

Brian K. Youngs, ND, DO,
Harrow, England

"I have used the Bach remedies regularly for over ten years, both personally and with patients. They have certainly proven their healing powers in accidents and for functional ailments and skin conditions."

K.J. Noblett, MB, ChB,
Blackpool, England

"I have used Rescue Remedy extensively in my chiropractic work, especially with patients in acute pain as a result of emotional distress. It helps amazingly in enabling patients to focus, listen to instructions, and relax— allowing the healing process to evolve. I have used [Rescue Remedy] personally in times of emotional crisis and have given it to my dog when she has been sick, always with positive results. It definitely allows for a calming and recentering, and I would be lost without it.

"Rescue Remedy cream has also been quite helpful in speeding the healing of abrasions and contusions as well as in relieving the joint pain of arthritis and bursitis in the acute phases. I use it automatically with my other modalities, like ultrasound and galvanic currents, in order to work it into the deeper tissues."

Barbara Dorf, DC,
Culver City, California

"I have been using the Bach Flower Remedies, including Rescue Remedy, for quite some years. I find them to be of remarkable service in stabilizing emotional upset during most traumatic situations. In our applied kinesiological testing, we have found the remedies to correct not just one, but three muscles (our criteria for their use), allowing a person to be more relaxed and receptive to other corrective procedures."

George Goodheart, DC,
Detroit, Michigan;
pioneer and developer of applied kinesiology;
author of numerous articles and text books
in the field of applied kinesiology

"I have used the Bach Flower Remedies, and the Rescue Remedy, [for] over thirty years, mostly for stress and emotional problems, with excellent results. A high percentage of patients, once they return to the office, report they are able to handle stress with much greater ease."

Harold J. Wilson, MD,
Columbus, Ohio

"In approximately ninety percent of the patients I've used the Bach Flower Remedies with, there has been a dramatic shift within a month in their basic attitudes toward themselves and others. This [shift] has resulted in greater self-acceptance and the realization that they are responsible for, and have control over, their own lives.

"I always use the Rescue Remedy when there's been any kind of accident that has resulted in emotional, psychological, or physical trauma. Following this, my patients have found that within a few hours, and most always within a few days, they have begun shaking off the effects of the accident."

Jeff Migdow, MD,
Kripalu Center, Lenox, Massachusetts

"The Bach Flower Remedies have been an integral part of my practice for the last two years, and the clinical results I have seen range from good to remarkable."

Louis I. Berlin, DC,
Atlanta, Georgia

"If I had to pick only one set of remedies of all the many systems of healing in the world, I would choose the Bach Flower Remedies alone. I believe these remedies to be many decades ahead of their time, and I am sure we will see a much more extensive use of them by doctors and the public alike. They have in some way a subtle effect on the inner self, often evinced quickly, whereas psychotherapy would have taken years, if ever, to achieve the same positive change."

C.K. Munro, MB, BAO,
Londonderry, Northern Ireland

"In my experience, the Bach Flower Remedies [chosen for the underlying emotional stress] have been helpful in classroom phobia, agoraphobia, sexual phobia, and premature ejaculation. The Rescue Remedy is good to start with for any anxiety, acute stress, and acute mental states. I've also seen Rescue Remedy alleviate tension in youngsters, especially before they take driving and classroom exams.

"I regard the Bach medicines as an essential extension of homoeopathic practice. One reason for this is that, unlike other homoeopathic medicines, they may be repeated, if necessary, with impunity. I highly recommend that every family have a bottle of Rescue Remedy, one for the home and another to be carried in their automobile for road emergencies."

Anthony D. Fox, MRCGP, DCH
Barton-on-Sea, England

"...I have used Rescue Remedy in many childbirth cases, always with satisfactory results. In some cases, I have recommended Rescue Remedy to women who were very nervous and uneasy about having natural childbirth. I suggested that they take it whenever they felt anxious during the days approaching delivery. Many did this and later shared with me how remarkably easy the births were. It is the single most important tool I carry in my treatment bag."

Marsha Woolf, ND,
Newton Corner, Massachusetts and
Providence, Rhode Island

"I have been using the Bach Flower Remedies for about seven years now and cannot imagine practicing without them. They continue to play an important and growing role, and sometimes their effects are astounding. Many patients tell me how remarkably positive their changes are after they begin using the remedies.

"I constantly use the Rescue Remedy in situations ranging from simple emotional upsets to heavy emotional trauma, with remarkable results. I also use the Rescue Remedy cream to massage onto bruises, bumps, tension headaches, and acute muscle and spinal pains with equally exceptional results."

Mark Smith, DC,
Vienna, Virginia

"I have had positive experiences with the Bach Flower Remedies. For example, I've treated a number of patients who have had a variety of gastrointestinal disorders, many of them long- standing. These individuals were helped dramatically by the Bach Flower Remedies. Though the remedies are not used specifically for physical ailments, in most cases where there is an underlying emotional problem, as there is in most [simple] gastrointestinal dysfunctions, we generally get excellent results."

Catherine Smith, MD,
Abingdon, Virginia

"I use the Bach Flower Remedies and Rescue Remedy in ninety percent of my practice, both before and after most dental procedures. I especially find them effective after surgery and reconstructive work and in easing the patients' trauma and stabilizing their condition.

"I find the Bach remedies and Rescue Remedy to be excellent for alleviating apprehension, both in adults and children, and especially for those suffering from temporal mandibular joint (TMJ) dysfunction. Many TMJ conditions are related to emotional imbalance, with fear a key element. There is not an emotionally based condition I have come across in my practice that the Bach Flower Remedies have not in some way been able to help. I wish that more dentists knew about the gentle yet consistently positive effects that the Bach remedies and Rescue Remedy have proven in my practice. If they did, they would not hesitate to use them themselves."

Maurice Tischler, DDS,
Woodstock, New York

"I have been using the Bach Flower Remedies for ten years as a part of my general medical practice. I have prescribed these remedies to well over two thousand patients and have found them to be of immense help in overcoming the negative emotional and mental states that seem to afflict us all.

"There is no doubt that the Bach remedies are capable of restoring the patient to emotional balance. The remedies, particularly the Rescue Remedy, are excellent in relieving acute states of distress resulting from sudden changes or catastrophes. The remedies also remove fear and anger and assist one in developing a more positive direction in life.

"I personally carry a bottle of Rescue Remedy with me at all times, and have used it during numerous emergencies, with immediate results. When grief occurs in the home, as from the loss of a dear one, there is no need for a potent sedative. Even here, Rescue Remedy proves extremely safe and effective.

"As a concerned physician, it is my hope that one day the Bach remedies will be a part of every doctor's healing practice."

Abram Ber, MD,
Phoenix, Arizona

"I have used the Bach remedies for nearly twenty years and have taken hundreds of patients off drugs (antidepressants, sedatives, tranquillizers) through their use. I use the remedies regularly at the Cancer Help Centre in Bristol, England, and find them to be most helpful in alleviating the emotional and psychological stress many of these patients experience. The remedies have also helped me personally through many family crisis situations as well. They are therapeutic agents I would never be without."

Alec Forbes, MD, FRCP,
formerly member, Expert Advisory Panel on
Traditional Medicine, World Health
Organization; medical director, Bristol Cancer
Help Centre, Bristol, England; author of
The Bristol Diet: Get Well and Eating Plan
(London: Century, 1984)

"I use the Rescue Remedy liquid concentrate internally, for calming emotional upset; and the liquid concentrate or cream externally, applied to lacerations or cuts, [this] seems to speed up the healing process. Often these wounds do not need to be sutured. A few drops of the remedy or application of the cream is all it takes. I find Rescue Remedy to be a very effective and powerful healing tool."

Joe D. Goldstrich, MD,
former medical director,
Pritikin Longevity Center,
Santa Monica, California;
author of *The Best Chance Diet*
(Atlanta: Humanics, 1982)

"In my former capacity as Dr. Margery Blackie's assistant [former physician to Her Majesty Queen Elizabeth II], both Dr. Blackie and I used the Rescue Remedy with very good results to treat people under stress. I have found it quite effective, without a doubt."

Charles K. Elliott, MB, BCh,
MFHom, MRCGP, MLCO, AFOM RCP,
London: Former Physician to Her Majesty Queen Elizabeth II;
co-editor of *Classical Homoeopathy* (Beaconsfield:
Beaconsfield Publishers Ltd., 1986)

"I have been using the Bach Flower Remedies primarily for insomnia, depression, and other nervous disorders and have found them to be extremely effective. I have found the Bach remedies, especially Rescue Remedy, to be valuable adjuncts to my homoeopathic practice."

Andrew H. Lockie, MRCGP, DObst RCOG,
Guildford, England

"I always keep a bottle of Rescue Remedy in my desk drawer for personal use and for friends and office staff, whenever there is any traumatic emotional or physical incident."

Richard Crews, MD, president,
Columbia Pacific University,
Mill Valley, California

"The Bach Flower Remedies are extremely sophisticated in their action. They are unusually gentle yet at the same time profoundly potent....I use the Bach Flower Remedies almost exclusively instead of tranquilizers and psychotropics, and I get excellent results. In many cases, they alleviate the problem when all else has failed."

J. Herbert Fill, MD, psychiatrist,
New York City, New York; former
New York City Commissioner of Mental Health;
author of *Mental Breakdown of a Nation*
(New York: Franklin Watts, 1974)

Emergencies: Professional and Consumer Use

The following section consists of emergency cases involving the professional and consumer use of Rescue Remedy. Emergencies are those situations that generally require immediate first aid or assistance.

Rescue Remedy is not meant to be a panacea or a substitute for emergency medical treatment. In all emergencies requiring medical attention, an ambulance or licensed physician should be called immediately.

Emergencies: Professional Use

"Recently, while traveling on a ship, I was called to treat a woman who wouldn't come out of her cabin. She was having an emotional crisis and was depressed and crying, saying she just couldn't face things. I administered a dose of Rescue Remedy and was then called away. One hour later, the woman approached me on deck, explaining how remarkably effective the remedy was in helping her overcome her terrible ordeal."

Alec Forbes, MD, FRCP,
Bristol, England

"We had just given a local anesthetic injection to a patient who told us that he didn't like Novocaine. Within a minute he began to shake and turn pale, apprehensive, and sweaty; he looked as though he were going to faint. I reached for the oxygen mask and the ammonia, but before I could get them to the patient my assistant had put four drops of Rescue Remedy liquid into the patient's half-open mouth. Instantly, he stopped shaking, his color returned, and he opened his eyes. He was completely recovered! Nothing but Rescue Remedy was used."

Steve Ross, DDS,
Wappinger Falls, New York

"A dentist friend and I were hiking in the woods when he was bitten by close to a hundred fire ants, over his arm and hands. These are extremely painful, itchy bites for most people, and my friend had been suffering for forty-five minutes before we were able to return to our cabin where I had some Rescue Remedy. If I had had the Rescue Remedy cream I would have used it, but since I didn't, I placed about ten to fifteen drops of Rescue Remedy liquid into a cup of spring water and applied this mixture to the bitten areas. Fire ant bites usually cause irritation to people for one to three days, or more. To our amazement, within a short time almost all itching, swelling, and inflammation ceased."

J. Hunter Lilly, ND, PhD,
Winter Haven, Florida

"During the first five days of an ocean voyage to Saudi Arabia, I was informed that a woman passenger was suffering from seasickness. I suggested to her husband that Rescue Remedy would be helpful for her. I gave him a bottle, instructing him to administer a dose under his wife's tongue every five minutes. Within the hour there was a marked improvement, and the next morning the woman was up and about, walking on deck. She had no recurrence of seasickness during the rest of the journey."

Ahmaed bin Embun, health practitioner,
Singapore, Malaysia

"I do chiropractic work with brain-damaged children, and many have responded well to Rescue Remedy. In several instances, these children were screaming and out of control when they came in for treatment. I administered a few drops of Rescue Remedy under their tongues, and their behavior improved immediately, like throwing a switch. It is quite amazing to watch."

Terry Franks, DC,
Burnsville, Minnesota

"One day, one of my patients who suffers from bouts of alcoholism came to see me. She was shaking, delirious, and completely out of control. During our two-hour session, I gave her repeated doses of liquid Rescue Remedy directly under her tongue. After the second dose, her tremors stopped, [and] she became increasingly coherent and able to function during the remaining part of the session. I gave her the rest of the bottle to take daily, which she did. Later that week at our next appointment, she said she felt better, and indeed she looked brighter than I had seen her look in a long time."

Joe Ann Cain, psychotherapist,
Encino, California

Emergencies: Consumer Use

I am a member of the Sri Chinmoy Marathon Team. After sixteen miles into a marathon, I usually become tired, irritable, and lightheaded. In my squirt bottle I carry a dilution of Rescue Remedy and water, which I usually drink during the last ten miles. It gives me energy and alleviates mental weariness and depression.

While running, I also apply Rescue Remedy cream to my knees to alleviate recurring pain, and I rub it on my calf muscles and ham strings, to relieve the muscle tightness I experience during the course of the race.

During my last race, I gave some Rescue Remedy cream to a friend who was also having knee pain midway through the race. A month before, he had had the same pain, and it had forced him to quit. This time, a few minutes after using the cream, he said his knee was fine. Following the race, he said he never would have finished if he hadn't used the Rescue Remedy.

Jamaica, New York

One day my sister and her son were digging a hole for a fence post. Accidentally she caught her leg in the equipment and ended up with a compound fracture. She quickly called out to her other son to bring the Rescue Remedy which was kept for emergencies. During the next five minutes, she promptly took repeated doses. The remedy immediately alleviated the worst effects of the trauma so that my sister was able to calmly organize her trip to the hospital.

Loudonville, New York

My oldest son cut his left thumb severely. Shortly after he became pale, dizzy, and nauseated, I gave him Rescue Remedy liquid orally and also applied it to the thumb full-strength and wrapped the finger with gauze. Within a short time my son's color returned, and he felt fine. No stitches were needed. He even complained afterwards about not having a scar to show for the cut.

Montgomery, Texas

I find the Rescue Remedy cream invaluable here in the tropical climate of Singapore, since cuts, wounds, or bruises sometimes take months to heal. The cream clears up a cut or bruise in one to two days.

Singapore, Malaysia

I used Rescue Remedy to counter my reaction to a skin cream, which had caused my eyes to become puffy and my face to become swollen and discolored. Hoping for relief, I first tried using a cold washcloth over my face; I also spent a lot of time in bed, dozing. In a couple of days, the redness and swelling abated, but my skin was scaly and itchy, as if I had a bad sunburn.

Then someone gave me some liquid Rescue Remedy, which I applied to my face several times. By evening I noticed a visible improvement, although I was still very anxious. The next morning, the improvement was more pronounced. I continued to apply the remedy every half-hour; at the end of the day not only was my anxiety gone, but I could see that my face was going to be all right.

Los Angeles, California

My mother recently slipped on a patch of ice in a parking lot, striking her head just above the temple, against the corner of a car. She blacked out completely for several seconds, then seemed to regain consciousness but was unable to say her name or respond in any way. She was very pale, as though in shock. I got her into the car, covered her with a blanket, and then gave her several drops of Rescue Remedy liquid which I always carry.

The effect was immediate. She became more conscious and asked for another dose. She was able to respond to questions, and although she still felt cold, her condition began to stabilize. Not surprisingly, she had a very bad headache. Seeing that she was okay, I took her home, where she soaked in a hot bath laced with a dropper full of Rescue Remedy. The next day her headache was almost gone, and she was able to go to work. Besides a chiropractic adjustment, no further treatment was needed.*

Ballston Lake, New York

---

*Blows to the head may result in a fracture or other complications, in all conditions requiring medical attention a physician should be consulted immediately.

One month ago, after carelessly touching a hot oven and burning myself, I immediately plunged my scorched hand into a jar of Rescue Remedy cream. Additionally, I took the liquid remedy as I massaged the cream onto the burned area. The next day I put in a twelve-hour shift at the hospital where I work as a nurse. My hands were constantly in and out of water, but there was no tenderness, just a slight redness. I continued to apply Rescue Remedy to the burned spot, and within one week I could not even see where the burn had been.

Kansas City, Missouri

Quite recently, while doing some work in my home, I hit my thumb with a hammer. The pain was very bad, and a throbbing sensation quickly developed in the thumb. My wife applied Rescue Remedy cream, and within moments the pain and throbbing were almost gone. It was quite remarkable.

We also use the Rescue Remedy with our children; it always seems to bring relief and comfort to them following their usual mishaps.

Kent, England

Our six-month-old baby had an injury on the foreskin of his penis—a painful place! He cried every time he urinated. We decided to try the Rescue Remedy and gave him four drops in some water orally, at the same time applying the Rescue Remedy cream to the injury. Our son fell into a sound and peaceful sleep almost immediately. After a few more applications over the next two days, the injury healed completely.

East Hampton, New York

When my four-year-old grandchild was bitten behind the ear by a dog, I immediately gave the child and his mother some Rescue Remedy, since they were both badly shaken. They became visibly calm within moments as preparations for emergency care were being made.

Tipp City, Ohio

Last summer, I was cutting hedges when a large branch flew up in my face, pushing my upper tooth through a half-inch of my lower lip, which started bleeding quite a bit. I held open the wound while my husband put two drops of full-strength Rescue Remedy on it. The bleeding slowed, and after several repeated doses over the next ten minutes it stopped completely. The wound healed in one week. Although I still have a knot in my lip, there is no scar at all.

Hull, Georgia

Preparing for extensive dental surgery, my wife put twenty drops of Rescue Remedy into a glass of water, which she sipped throughout the day before and after her surgery. She did not feel any pain on the day of surgery or on the days following it, nor did she have to take any codeine or aspirin. Sleep came naturally and easily without medication that first night and on the following nights as well. My wife visited the dental surgeon two days after the surgery, and he was astounded at how quickly she had healed.

California

We couldn't get through a summer without the Rescue Remedy ointment. It instantly relieves all types of insect stings.

Washington, D.C.

One night my husband began hemorrhaging. The amount of blood he was vomiting terrified both of us. I gave him some Rescue Remedy as soon as he could keep it down, and he was soon able to walk calmly out of the bathroom. I'm a nurse, so I know that in a situation like this it is imperative that the patient be calmed. I also took a dose of Rescue Remedy myself every ten or fifteen minutes so that I, too, could stay calm. It helped us both very much; I was easily able to get my husband to the emergency room without either of us panicking.

Salisbury, North Carolina

My husband and I went for a long drive last week and were badly shaken up by a near-accident. The car ahead of us stopped very suddenly, and my husband jammed on the brakes just in time. We were very shaken, but we put some drops of the Rescue Remedy on our tongues and were genuinely surprised at the speed which it worked and with which our nervousness disappeared.

California

My friend and I used Rescue Remedy to help ourselves get through a rough climb up Mount Cruach Ardrain, in Scotland. About halfway up, it began to get very cold, and we became extremely exhausted. But we knew we had to continue if we were going to complete the climb. I took a sip from the small bottle of Rescue Remedy that I had in my coat and told my companion that he must take some if we were to make it through the climb. After remaining motionless for a few minutes, we felt sufficiently recovered to complete a final patch, returning safely, in a time that was something of a record. I am quite certain that we would not have completed that climb had it not been for the Rescue Remedy.

Scotland

One of the students in my cooking class cut her finger quite badly. Despite our prompting she refused to go to a doctor, and rather than argue with her, I gave her several drops from my Rescue Remedy bottle. I also had her lie down, and packed her finger with Rescue Remedy cream. This dressing I changed every few hours. The next day, the wound was still open but looking pink and alive. I put on a new dressing and told my student to change it every day. When she showed it to me four days later, I couldn't believe my eyes. The skin had completely healed; there wasn't even a line where it had been cut. Except for the fact that my student's nail was partially gone, there was no sign of the wound.

Amsterdam, Holland

My five-year-old niece fell off her bicycle, tearing skin off her nose, bruising both lips badly, and leaving a front tooth dangling. She screamed with pain as we squirted some Rescue Remedy straight into her mouth and headed for the nearest hospital. The remedy didn't seem to have any effect on her. We gave her a few more doses while waiting for the doctor, but that didn't help. Then it dawned on me that she was spitting blood—and the Rescue Remedy along with it. I immediately started applying the drops behind her ears, and the result was almost instantaneous; my niece stopped screaming and became very cooperative. The look of disbelief on the nurse's face was an absolute study.

In another incident: I gashed my left hand with a can opener, near the joint between the thumb and index finger. The cut was deep and half an inch long. I applied Rescue Remedy cream immediately and then covered my hand with a Band-Aid. Three days later, I found that the cut was healing. I took off the covering on the fifth day, and all that was left was a little scar. This surprised me greatly, since other cuts I've had have always healed extremely slowly.

Victoria, Australia

I burned the inside of my mouth with some very hot food. I have done this before and usually it means agony for at least two days and discomfort for another week or two. This time I rubbed some Rescue Remedy liquid on the burned spot and got relief within seconds. I applied a few more doses; before the day was over, the pain was gone.

London, England

I am physically handicapped from polio and have to walk with crutches. One day, while reaching for a jar on a high shelf, I stretched too far and felt a sudden, violent pain in my middle finger and my wrist. My hand became swollen and remained painful for the next ten days; gradually, it started to become numb.

On the tenth day I saw my doctor, who became concerned because the finger was not only swollen but was starting to curve in. An X-ray, however, showed nothing wrong. Ten days later—my hand still hurting—a friend suggested that I try my Rescue Remedy. I immediately put the cream on the finger, and in about two hours the pain was virtually gone. At this time I again applied more cream, and the next morning the pain and swelling were all but gone. I was able to stretch my hand and fingers normally. It was miraculous. Neither the pain nor the swelling has returned since then.

Herefordshire, England

A young girl of seven with a history of travel sickness was due to go on a holiday to Spain. Her parents, who were worried that they had to journey for three hours in a bus before they reached their destination, had asked if I had any ideas which might help. I suggested the girl use the Rescue Remedy, which I knew to be somewhat effective in these circumstances, along with the Bach remedy Scleranthus. After obtaining a mixture, the mother later told me that she had administered it frequently, both before and during the trip, which proceeded without any mishap whatsoever.

Pinner, England

Whenever I go to San Francisco, I spend half my time soaking my hot, swollen feet, which can't seem to take the constant trudging up and down the steep hills. Last time, however, I obtained and smoothed on the Rescue Remedy cream. The relief was immediate. The heat left my feet at once, and the swelling was reduced shortly thereafter. I continued to use the Rescue Remedy during the rest of my trip and was not bothered with foot problems for the remainder of my stay.

Everett, Washington

After a recent operation, I found it difficult to sleep. I would jerk and toss continuously. My various surgical wounds hurt me, and my brain seemed to be on fire. At one point, my wife gave me a dose of Rescue Remedy; within minutes I quieted down, shortly afterwards falling into a peaceful sleep. It was miraculous.

For two days and nights I was able to lie still. I was so tranquil that the bed clothes were left undisturbed. My mind was at peace, and I lay contentedly, not reading and rarely speaking, just enjoying the peace. By the third day, I was feeling much better and more relaxed. The Bach remedies have helped me tremendously.

USA

I was working on a fluorescent fixture and did not know that someone had forgotten to turn off the power. After grabbing the exposed wires, I got an intense electrical shock. Quite shaken up, I located my bottle of Rescue Remedy and immediately took four drops under my tongue, and several more within the next half-hour. The effects of the shock disappeared within minutes; in a half-hour, I was fine.

Philadelphia, Pennsylvania

Emotional and Psychological Stress: Professional and Consumer Use

The following section consists of cases specifically involving the use of Rescue Remedy for acute emotional and psychological stress.

Emotional and psychological stress includes, but is not limited to anxiety, nervousness, panic, and non-clinical depression. The stress may result from everyday situations, such as visiting a dentist, taking an exam, receiving bad news, or as a result of accidents.

Emotional and Psychological Stress: Professional Use

"I have my patients sip Rescue Remedy in warm water, and it always seems to calm them. One very disturbed patient, who had been on numerous tranquilizers with poor results, described to me his experience with the Rescue Remedy. He stated that Rescue Remedy assisted him in feeling calm and natural, and that it has helped him more than anything else he has ever tried for his nervous condition."

Catherine R. Smith, MD,
Abingdon, Virginia

"I prescribe Rescue Remedy liquid for the sense of internal panic brought on by the diagnosis of cancer. It helps both the patient and family cope more easily with the situation. In the acute phase of bereavement, Rescue Remedy is of definite value. One man whose thirty-two-year-old wife had suddenly died used Rescue Remedy as often as every two hours for many weeks and reported that it always eased his panic and tears.

"Rescue Remedy is excellent as a convalescent tonic, when given [four] drops four times daily, especially for the elderly."

D.T.H. Williams, MB, DObst RCOG,
Chiddingfold, Surrey, England

"Recently, a thirty-seven-year-old woman who was attempting to reduce a sixteen-year dependency on Valium came to see me. Withdrawal was causing her extreme pain in her muscles and joints, and feelings of suffocation. She had already seen several physicians who offered her no relief. I suggested that she try the Bach Rescue Remedy. After five to six doses at fifteen-minute intervals before bedtime, she would sleep quite well. After taking Rescue Remedy for two months, along with counseling during the crisis periods, she has considerably reduced her Valium intake, along with her extreme tension and worry. Now, after further Bach remedies, and counseling, she has been off Valium for over a year."

Doug Lancaster, health practitioner,
Kingston, Ontario, Canada

"An extremely depressed thirty-eight-year-old man came to me for treatment; he was nervous, exhausted, unclean, and was exacerbating his problems by smoking two to three packs of cigarettes a day. He had very low self-esteem worsened by his feeling that he lacked sufficient will-power to control his smoking.

"I gave him one dose of the Rescue Remedy at the beginning of our session, and he sat for three hours without reaching for a cigarette. He said it was the first time in years he hadn't felt like smoking.... [Following our session he later reported] that after taking the Rescue Remedy for just a short time he had begun to develop a much deeper level of self-respect and a greater sense of well-being."

Loretta Hilsher, PhD, DN,
president and founder of
Hyperactive Children's Institute,
Chicago, Illinois

"In our office we have a dropper bottle of Rescue Remedy by each chair. Before any injection or stressful treatment, we give the patient a few drops of the remedy. We explain to the patient that the Rescue Remedy is a helpful, herbal remedy without side effects. We find that the Rescue Remedy helps raise a patient's resistance to stress while at the same time having a great calming influence. We have also adopted a policy of offering a bottle of Rescue Remedy to any patient we refer to an oral surgeon or endodontist."

Jerry Mittelman, DDS,
New York City, New York

"I treated a violinist who had severe stage fright before a performance, feeling that she could not go on. I gave her some Rescue Remedy to take before going on stage, and now she says she actually enjoys performing.

"Another musician, who plays the flute, said she would be tense for two weeks before a performance. For a while, regular doses of Rescue Remedy during the days before a concert made her performances better, her experiences exciting and enjoyable. Now she finds she feels this way with only a few doses prior to a performance."

Jeff Migdow, MD,
Kripalu Center, Lenox, Massachusetts

"A forty-nine-year-old client went through a traumatic divorce, lost his medical practice, and had an emotional and physical breakdown. Though various kinds of treatments have helped him, he still has occasional periods of great emotional agitation. During these episodes, Rescue Remedy improves his ability to function and to continue his work day."

David Winston, nutritional consultant,
Franklin Park, New Jersey

Emotional and Psychological Stress: Consumer Use

A month ago my sister rammed into a Coca-Cola truck with her new VW. I received a call from the hospital and got very nervous and shaky. Immediately I took four drops of Rescue Remedy; very quickly I stopped shaking and was able to turn my attention to my sister's well-being.

Upon my arrival at the hospital I found that my sister had only minor cuts and bruises, but she was emotionally out of control. She was crying and hysterical, worried about our parents' reproaches and her unpaid-for car. I gave her a dose of Rescue Remedy, and she immediately stopped crying. With a deep breath, she relaxed and closed her eyes. Fifteen minutes later, she was anxious again, so I repeated the dose. We continued in this way for an hour and a half.

My sister was released from the hospital, laughing and back to her old self. There was no further need for the remedy after that, and within a week the cuts and bruises were completely healed.

New Mexico

The local bakery burned down a few weeks ago. When my friend, who lives next door to the baker, went in to see if she could help, she found the baker's wife completely traumatized. My friend immediately gave her two or three doses of Rescue Remedy; within a short time, the woman was back to her normal self. Her colour had completely returned, and she has not shown any signs of disturbance since then.

Ascot, England

A Japanese passenger sitting alongside us on a recent airplane trip was obviously terrified. His body was doubled up, his head buried in his hands, his meal untouched. We gave him a few drops of Rescue Remedy in water, and he became relaxed almost immediately; he soon fell asleep. He awoke quite a long time afterwards and ate the next meal quite well. Since he spoke no English, he passed on his grateful thanks for the special 'medicine' via a bilingual hostess.

Australia

I am a registered nurse working in an in-patient mental health facility. I began using Rescue Remedy regularly in February 1981, when I was a medical staff nurse under a great deal of stress. At the time, I was close to a nervous breakdown, suffering from what was eventually diagnosed as adrenal exhaustion and hypoglycemia. For several months, in addition to experiencing insomnia and depression, I would feel extremely anxious and panic-stricken whenever my blood sugar fluctuated. I used the Rescue Remedy many times throughout this period to alleviate my feelings of panic and acute anxiety. It seemed to help stabilize both my mind and my body.

Moreover, I feel that the Rescue Remedy has been invaluable to my personal growth and transformation, helping me gain a greater sense of understanding and self-awareness throughout some rough periods in my life.

Fort Wayne, Indiana

My youngest son, now six-years-old, used to be a thin, emotional child, at times very sweet and reasonable, at other times a holy terror. Touchy and sensitive, he would sometimes have a screaming tantrum over nothing. I ordered some Rescue Remedy liquid, and during the next emotional outburst I gave him four drops. Within five minutes, right before our eyes, he calmed down; his face softened and became rounded, and his demeanor changed so much that my fourteen-year-old son exclaimed, 'If it will do that for him, fix me some.'

Montgomery, Texas

Recently, my three-year-old daughter had to have a front tooth refilled. We gave her a dose of Rescue Remedy just before going to the dentist. Both my wife and the doctor were amazed at how thoroughly calm and cooperative she was throughout the process. Even while the dentist used his drill, my daughter never once winced or cried.

Mount Shasta, California

Recently, two of my friends were in similar situations of breaking up with their mates and experiencing severe emotional trauma. I gave each of them a bottle of Rescue Remedy and told them to take doses daily. Afterwards, they both reported feeling much calmer and told me how the remedy helped them through their difficult periods.

San Diego, California

Some friends of mine made the difficult decision to divorce. When they told their twelve-year-old son, he became extremely upset and frightened. He paced around, shouting and crying, hitting the walls and furniture. His mother gave him several doses of Rescue Remedy, and within twenty minutes he calmed down and was able to discuss the situation rationally.

Albuquerque, New Mexico

A young Indian girl, frightened by her first menstrual period, became deeply disturbed after a friend laughed at her and told her that she should be ashamed of herself for bleeding. For two weeks, the girl sat in a dark corner, crying and refusing to speak to anyone, even her mother. Doctors were treating the girl with vitamins and tranquilizers, but to no avail.

Fortunately, when I arrived on the scene, I had my little bottle of Rescue Remedy, and since the mother had lost faith in the treatment applied so far, she agreed to put the remedy to the test. After the first day, the girl started to speak. On the fourth day after her treatment with Rescue Remedy, the girl was completely well; she did not cry, and she said she no longer felt afraid.

Honduras

Recently, I moved from suburbia to my dream house in the mountains. While moving, I experienced total physical exhaustion, financial disaster, confusion, burnout, and sheer terror, along with an indescribable feeling of elation and joy. Close to a complete nervous breakdown, I began taking Rescue Remedy every five minutes. Within a short time, I noticed a core of strength that I had never realized before. My emotions evened out, and I felt an inner calm and a renewed self-control emerging.

Santa Barbara, California

While I was going through an intensive, five-day personal-growth training program, I began to feel a great deal of stress. Also, since the sessions lasted from early in the morning to late at night, I was getting very little sleep. I decided to try the Rescue Remedy, and after taking regular doses for about three days, I noticed a sense of well-being that surprised me. The remedy definitely helped stabilize my emotions during a particularly rough period in my personal life.

Philadelphia, Pennsylvania

As a rule, I am terribly nervous when I have to speak in public. However, the last lecture I gave was a wonderful experience. I took a dose of the Rescue Remedy upon waking that day, another at midday, and one just before I went on the platform. To my surprise and delight, I had no dry lips or butterflies in my stomach and not a twinge of fear.

Sussex, England

My whole family took Rescue Remedy every day during the first month of mourning after my mother died. It didn't change the quality of our grief, but we were able to deal with it and accept what had happened more easily.

Newton Corner, Massachusetts

Rescue Remedy has come to my rescue many times. However, my favorite Rescue Remedy story happened when my new car was stolen. I was at a gas station, paying for my gas, when two boys jumped into my car and drove off. My purse, along with my Rescue Remedy, was on the front seat. Standing there, feeling shocked and confused, I became outraged when I realized that they had stolen my Rescue Remedy, and I needed it!

Miami, Florida

In addition to being a nutritionist, I'm an actress working on a show right now. I have a highly emotional presentation at the end of scene two, which is immediately followed by a scene showing me four days later, happy and carefree. Rescue Remedy is the only thing that calms me down during the transition between scenes. I exit from one side of the stage, shaking and crying, walk around the other side of the theater, pass my dressing room, take my Rescue Remedy and three deep breaths, and go on in the next scene, relaxed and happy.

New York City, New York

My flatmate and I are both policewomen. We once interviewed a rape victim who had great difficulty recalling specific details of her recent ordeal. My partner gave the woman a dose of Rescue Remedy, and the change was almost immediate. The sequence of events became coherent, an excellent statement was obtained, and the victim's very accurate description of the offender led to his arrest a short time later.

Victoria, Australia

One of my twelve-year-old pupils played the goal position on our school football team. Before each game he would become quite upset and nervous, since the boys would tease him if he let the ball through the goal. Though skeptical, he finally agreed to sip some Rescue Remedy two hours before our next game. The following day I was thrilled when this very skeptical child, grinning from ear to ear, stated before the class, 'Your magic stuff is great; I wasn't nervous at all, even when I did let the ball go through.'

London, England

My children take Rescue Remedy before their college tests and just before their on-stage performances in order to offset anxiety. I take it before I meditate; it helps me to release my stress, relax, and enhance my experience.

New York City, New York

At the hotel where I was staying in Iona, I had great success with the Bach Flower Remedies, particularly the Rescue Remedy. Four visitors arrived, disoriented and suffering from exposure after the engine of their boat had broken down during a storm. I was able to give two of them the Rescue Remedy, and their recovery was amazing. They were calm within a matter of hours, while the other two poor souls had to be confined for two to three days.

Isle of Iona, Scotland

Two children had lost their mother to cancer. The youngest was four, the oldest eight. After the funeral, their father complained that the older girl was suddenly afraid of the dark and could not sleep through the night without wetting her bed, an unusual habit for her. She had nightmares three or four times a week and thus continued to worry her father. Her younger sister also cried incessantly and had nightmares. I gave both children Rescue Remedy.

Additionally, I suggested that their father give them both four drops of the Rescue Remedy each time they woke during the night and before meals during the day. Within three nights the bed-wetting stopped, and both children slept peacefully.

Sante Fe, New Mexico

During a meeting at our Urban Health Center, seven or eight children, all strangers to one another, began to fight and cry, and the mothers responded with angry slaps and reprimands. To try and settle the furor, I gave everyone a dose of liquid Rescue Remedy. Within just a few minutes, peace and harmony were restored.

Chicago, Illinois

I noticed a woman waiting outside the intensive care unit where her mother was dying. She was in semi-shock, quite anxious and very cold. I handed her a small bottle of Rescue Remedy and told her how to use it. She began taking the liquid, and it seemed to relax her very soon after; she seemed able to accept the situation a little more calmly.

Salisbury, North Carolina

I took the Rescue Remedy before taking an exam and found it extremely helpful. I normally waste a lot of time deciding which questions to answer and what to write. But this time, I was able to write quickly, and I felt quite alert and tranquil.

England

Some severe personal problems caused me to have acute anxiety attacks nearly every day. These attacks were no doubt aggravated by my quitting smoking. To control the anxiety, I started taking tranquilizers on and off for a year. Also, for two previous years I'd had dizzy spells whose cause no doctor could find. The day I took my first dose of Rescue Remedy was the last day I needed a tranquilizer. As I continued to take the Rescue Remedy, my anxiety attacks slowly abated, then disappeared, as did my dizzy spells.

New York City, New York

Pregnancy and Childbirth:
Professional and Consumer Use

The Bach Flower Remedies can be particularly helpful before and throughout pregnancy, as well as during childbirth, when a prospective mother's moods fluctuate more than usual. Since the moods are distinctly defined, they can be treated by the mother-to-be herself or by her adviser. A quiet, happy frame of mind is one of the greatest contributors to a painless and easy birth. In addition to being taken internally, Rescue Remedy can be applied externally to the wrist, temples, and navel of the newborn, when and as needed.

The Bach Flower Remedies, as well as Rescue Remedy, have also been shown to be especially valuable in dealing with children's emotional difficulties—for example, fear and restlessness—before more complex patterns have a chance to develop.

In addition, Dr. John Diamond, a psychiatrist and well-known author, in his introduction to *Handbook of the Bach Flower Remedies*, by Philip Chancellor (New Canaan: Keats, 1980), states: "The Bach remedies have tremendous power for good and are completely free of any harmful effects." This is especially important, because many substances commonly used today for most emotional difficulties have warnings about repetition and dosage.

Because of recent FDA regulations, most over-the-counter drugs require a warning for pregnant women regardless of the drug's toxicity. *It is important to check with your physician before taking any form of medication during pregnancy.* However no known side effects have been attributed to the Bach Flower Remedies or to Rescue Remedy in over fifty years of use.

Pregnancy and Childbirth: Professional Use

"Our hospital's doctor, not able to find the cause of the illness, had done all he could for a six-week-old baby who was failing quickly. Based on my experience in emergency situations, I decided to start the infant on Bach Rescue Remedy; the effect was profound. From that point on, her condition took a dramatic shift in a positive direction. The doctor could hardly believe it when a week later, the baby's condition appeared to be stabilized."

Sister Natalie, superintendent,
St. John's Hospital, Poona, India

"While I was attending a thirty-four-year-old woman who was in the second stage of labour, she was having extreme contractions. The fetal heart monitor indicated that the fetus was in distress. The patient was getting hysterical, and we were considering a Caesarean section. I applied Rescue Remedy to her lips from a cloth three times within a fifteen-minute period. The fetal heartbeat evened out, the contractions were much milder, and the whole labour process stopped for about two hours. The woman calmed down and actually slept. When she awoke, labour began again, and there was a normal delivery, with no further complications or distress."

In another case: "I was in attendance when a child was born at home, the umbilical cord twisted twice around his neck. Since the cord was too tight, it was necessary to cut and clamp it immediately. The child was not breathing, his vital signs were low, and he displayed a poor colour. We rubbed Rescue Remedy all over his face. Within a short period, though it seemed forever, he started breathing, and his normal responses quickly picked up."

Gretchen Lawlor, ND,
Tunbridge Wells, England

"Recently, I was called to the hospital where one of my maternity patients had a series of minor convulsions directly preceding her labour. When I arrived, I immediately swabbed her tongue and inside her lips with Rescue Remedy. The convulsions ceased, and I left her drinking water 'doctored' with the Rescue Remedy. I continued this treatment throughout the next day and the following morning. Later that day, my patient delivered the child, with no discomfort."

Dr. T. L.
Northampton, England

"A fifteen-month-old-girl running a high fever was recently brought to me. I applied Rescue Remedy cream to various parts of her body, and within half an hour she was fast asleep, and her fever dropped. Two days later, she had fully recovered. I've used Rescue Remedy cream and drops in similar cases of fever in children, always with good results."

Ahmaed bin Embun, health practitioner,
Singapore, Malaysia

"I recently attended a twenty-one-year-old woman who was in labour at West London Hospital with her first child. Since she was quite agitated, I administered a dose of Rescue Remedy to calm her during the second stage and especially during the transition period of labour. She had a unusually easy birth without any complications, which I attributed to the Rescue Remedy."

Sarah Moon, BAc,
London, England

"Very shortly after her daughter was born, my patient nearly passed out. Since there were complications and a lot of bleeding, I gave her a dose of Rescue Remedy, which, within moments, brought her back to clarity. The rapidity of recovery was quite amazing to witness."

G. S. Khalsa, MD,
Lathrup Village, Michigan

"A thirty-one-year-old woman patient of mine had wanted natural childbirth but was two weeks past her delivery date. She was taken to the hospital to have labour induced. This upset her. She had lower back pain; she was apprehensive, and she felt a sense of failure at not having a home birth.

"I gave her five drops of Rescue Remedy in warm water. There was an immediate dramatic change, and she said, 'I'm going to really cope with this.' She was suddenly clear and had her first baby in three hours."

Lorraine Taylor, BAc,
Oxford, England

"Recently, I gave Rescue Remedy to a young woman in the early stages of labour. She was highly nervous, but after a few sips of the remedy in water she calmed down considerably. After ten minutes, her contractions regulated and labour progressed beautifully. She gave birth within two hours in a relaxed and normal manner. Also, as a preventative to postnatal depression, there is nothing equal to Rescue Remedy."

E. Eckstein, RMH*,
England

Pregnancy and Childbirth: Consumer Use

The following letter was written to John Ramsell who, with his sister, Nickie Murray, carries on Dr. Bach's work as the current curators of the Bach Centre in England. The letter eventually appeared in *Mothering* magazine, Spring 1983, and is printed here with permission from the

* Registered Medical Herbalist

writer. An extremely moving account of one woman's coura-
geous battle to save her child, the letter is included here so
that the reader may share in the woman's experience. **No
medical claims are implied or made here for the Bach remedies or Rescue Remedy, in Down's Syndrome, or any other
serious medical disorder by either the author or the publisher.**

Dear John,

I knew I would have a story to tell, but I had no idea it
would be so dramatic. You might just want to put your feet
up in one of those wonderful wooden chairs Dr. Edward
Bach built, to read this one.

I had made about eight one-ounce dropper bottles full of
my favorite Bach flowers—Rescue Remedy, Walnut, Mimulus, and Oak—the day my labor began. I took them regularly on my tongue, and put four or five drops on the crown
of my head to even out the rough edges. I was 9¾ cm. dilated when my labor stopped...thirty-six long, long hours
later.

Since I had planned a home delivery, I did my laboring at
home to the hour. Soon, I figured the son within me was not
safe in his own right; otherwise, he would have been born by
then. I got my bag, and off to the hospital I went with my
husband, my midwives, my remedies, and the baby still
within. I slipped a bottle of comfrey and chlorophyll into my
medicine pouch and thought I was ready.

When I arrived at the hospital, I had a heavy contraction
at the front desk, and the woman there screamed, "Are you
going to have your baby right here? Right now? Get into a
wheelchair and use the service elevator—it's faster!"

A fetal monitor determined that baby Anton was in distress—imagine having one's head caught in the cervix for
thirty-six hours—and we opted for a Caesarean section. It
was performed at 9 p.m.—eight long hours later.

The remedy I continued to take every three minutes in
front of all the attending doctors and nurses kept them very

curious. When asked by my doctor what I was so faithfully taking, I told him it was a remedy for impatience. He laughed, and admitted that he, too, could probably use some, although he never asked to try any.

Baby Anton was born in distress. He had no lung capacity and swallowed meconium (baby's first elimination) after my waters broke early in the morning. The heart had enlarged to keep the baby alive. He was put on 100% oxygen immediately, and he looked as if he wanted to go back to the garden.

About ten minutes out of recovery, our pediatrician told us our son was born with Down's Syndrome. In addition, he had many problems and had about two hours to live. Did we want to see him? Yes, Did we make funeral arrangements at the pediatricians suggestion? Yes, we did that too. We cried mostly; this was a little much to bear, even with the remedies. I asked my husband to return home and bring back the entire set of thirty-eight remedies. I added the Bach flower Gorse...[for hopelessness] to our remedy, and we took it continually. Soon, we calmed down.

I was wheeled into Infant Intensive Care where I could not reach my son's head after my own abdominal surgery. I asked my husband to put Oak, Walnut, and Rescue Remedy on his (the baby's) knees, feet, and chest—between the EKG and catheter wires. If our son was going to die, I wanted his transition to be a peaceful one. I knew the flower Walnut would aid his transition. We told the nurses it was holy water. Even though they were incredible women, I figured the chances of their knowing about the Bach flowers were ten to one. I felt too weak to explain.

The pediatricians said they would transport baby Anton to a large city hospital sixty miles away. They would be "better equipped" there to save his life, if in fact it could be saved. Heart surgery would probably also be necessary. Jack and I said no, no, no to both....If baby Anton was to live, he would have to pull through where he was born, here in the mountains of this small city.

That night, I stayed with him in intensive care and reached into his oxygen tent, scared to death he might die if I opened it up. I fed him my remedy, now his, through an eyedropper. He was so dehydrated he slurped it up with all the enthusiasm he could gather. Every ten minutes I gave him his remedy: on the knees, his mouth, and on the crown of his badly misshapen head. I did this for twenty-four hours. The Newborn Nursery nurses kept him warm and dry and untangled from all those wires. Then I went to bed.

When I woke the next day, eight hours later, I slightly remember the doctor saying the crisis seemed to be over. We then administered an intense stimulation program. Soon, I could hold my son with blow-by oxygen in between the wires. He had a strong suck, and breast-fed in six or seven days. Little by little, over a ten-day period in intensive care, we used six ounces of remedy. The oxygen supply was decreased from 100% eventually to room air. I added tincture of comfrey and chlorophyll to my milk. Baby's skin was rubbed down with the gel from live Aloe Vera plants three or four times every twelve hours. He was three weeks overdue, and he looked as if he had spent that time in a bathtub. His head shaped up. His skin is beautiful. We have a baby boy.

We continue our daily use of the Bach flowers. Thanks again for carrying on Bach's work. In the eight years I have used these remedies, I have never been so appreciative that Bach discovered them. With my thanks, please expect a package of herbal teas for you and all your staff, and your guests from the world over.

Most sincerely,

Alexandra Kolkmeyer
Author of *A Modern Woman's Herbal*
(Santa Fe, New Mexico: Insight Press, 1976)

Since the birth of my first child eleven years ago was such a painful and frightening experience, I grew quite terrified as the time came closer for my second child to be born. However, following sound advice, I took Rescue Remedy during labour, and the delivery was quick and easy. I became quite relaxed both during and after the birth.

Isles of Scilly, England

When the third member of our family arrived early this summer, it became evident to me that the Rescue Remedy was also the baby's remedy. I found it a wonderful and almost instantaneous cure for colic.

Three drops in a tablespoon of warm boiled water worked like magic.

Selsdon, England

Before delivering her baby, my daughter regularly took Rescue Remedy, and her labour only lasted an hour and a half. The nurses said they had never seen such a quick and easy delivery, and called her son Speedy Gonzales. She is continuing with the remedy and is so relieved that this baby, as opposed to her first, sleeps peacefully through the night.

Devon, England

I began taking Rescue Remedy with the onset of labour contractions while on the way to the hospital. The contractions started coming every three minutes, and by the time I arrived I was fully dilated and ready to push. In the delivery room my husband gave me water with the Bach Flower Rescue Remedy added. Between each contraction, I was fully aware of all that was going on. Even through the powerful contractions I had no need for painkillers and after an hour gave birth to twin boys.

I took Rescue Remedy throughout my six days in the hospital by putting a few drops in my bedside water. This helped me to cope with the overwhelming task of breastfeeding two hungry babies. I attributed the calmness and inner strength I felt throughout this intense experience to Dr. Bach's Rescue Remedy.

Derbyshire, England

"My first birth was a nightmare. There's no other word for it. Even the midwife, who attended as one of my coaches, admitted that it was 'one of the more difficult' she had seen. ... No, I was not medicated, and yes, I was a 'prepared' woman. But prepared for what? After twenty-four hours of excruciating back labor, with little or no dilation, no breathing technique could alleviate the pain and exhaustion I was suffering....

"Sensing my panic, my coach pulled a small bottle of Rescue Remedy, a Bach flower extract, from her pocket and dripped three or four drops of the dew-like liquid into my mouth.... Soon after that, an unexpected surge of energy and concentration came over me. After three long pushes, my baby girl emerged in one sudden, hot, wet 'plop.'...

"...When things got bad [during my second birth], I asked my other coach for the Rescue Remedy."

Olympia, Washington (Extracted from *Mothering* magazine, Spring 1984)

Recently, I suggested Rescue Remedy to a young woman in the early stages of labour. She was highly nervous, but after a few sips of the remedy in water she calmed down considerably. After ten minutes, her contractions regulated and labor progressed beautifully. She gave birth within two hours in a relaxed and normal manner. Also, as a preventive to postnatal depression, there is nothing equal to Rescue Remedy.

England

I was ten weeks pregnant when I started to miscarry. I began to bleed so profusely that I almost passed out. All I had time to say was, 'Get the Rescue Remedy off the shelf!' I took it every few moments until I regained my strength and was able to get medical assistance. The bleeding lessened a bit, and I was able to get to the hospital in a stable condition. Rescue Remedy will always be on hand in my home for any emergency.

New South Wales, Australia

Following a loss in the family, my stress was compounded by an ectopic pregnancy [in the Fallopian tube], which had aborted. This was followed by surgical removal of the damaged tube and ovary as well. During this period, Rescue Remedy was the only thing that kept me [emotionally] stable. Shortly after my return from the hospital, my marriage began to break up, and once again Rescue Remedy proved invaluable in helping me through this time.

I have used all the Bach remedies, and they have played an important role in helping me cope with the changes I've experienced in my life. They have allowed me to change my negative thoughts and thus develop more fully as a human being. I cannot speak highly enough of Dr. Bach and his remedies.

Lancashire, England

After much debating, we took our two-month-old daughter to receive her first immunization vaccine. The after effects of this shot were dreadful. The poor little baby ran a high fever and went into a frenzy, screaming for hours. Before her second shot, we rubbed Rescue Remedy cream on the spot where the needle would go in, and she didn't feel a thing. For the rest of the day, we gave her Rescue Remedy orally, and this time she had no after effects whatsoever. We dealt with the third shot the same way, and our daughter actually seemed to enjoy her visit with the doctor.

USA

Acute and Chronic: Professional and Consumer Use

The following section consists of cases involving the professional and consumer use of Rescue Remedy for acute and chronic conditions. Acute conditions are defined here as those conditions that appear suddenly but do not require emergency assistance. Chronic conditions are those a person has lived with over a long period of time.

Acute and Chronic: Professional Use

"One of my patients was a thirty-six-year-old woman who was a heavy drinker and smoker with a history of chronic depression. I suggested that she take the Bach Flower Rescue Remedy, which she did. The next day, she reported that she had slept for the first time in two weeks and felt a sense of relief from her problems. She continued to take the remedy and after two or three weeks was able to stabilize her condition. She now takes the remedy intermittently."

Jeffrey Fine, ND, PhD,
Palm Beach Shores, Florida

"J.T. is a sixty-five-year-old ex-weight-lifter who had been having attacks of 'wooziness' and lightheadedness for the last year and a half. They would occur if he sat still for more than a half-hour or if he drove a car for over an hour and then stood up. He would then feel weak and tired for a few hours after the attack. When he came to my office, he had been seen by his family doctor, given tranquilizers and told 'to take it easy.'

"After talking with him and examining him, I suggested he take Rescue Remedy daily when these attacks occur. I also prescribed some vitamin supplements for stress. When I saw him next, he reported only two episodes in the intervening six weeks (he had been having them daily). At the beginning of both episodes, he had taken three drops of Rescue Remedy. He told me these drops seemed to clear up the wooziness quickly, and a full-blown attack never materialized.

"Additionally, he said that he knew things had changed when, during a recent bridge game, he got up to go to the kitchen after sitting for over two hours, (this normally would have created a problem for him) and became really excited when he realized that he had not been weak or woozy for weeks."

Ronald Dushkin, MD,
Kripalu Center, Lenox, Massachusetts

"A patient of mine was diagnosed as being severely hypoglycemic as well as having severe allergic responses to all kinds of foods and foreign proteins. The Rescue Remedy liquid has proven significant in terms of providing stress relief during the acute episodes, especially after [the patient takes] any offending substances."

Jim Said, DC, ND
Grants Pass, Oregon

Acute and Chronic: Consumer Use

I have suffered from head noises for forty years, and all the doctor and ear specialists I have seen have been of little help. Two nights ago, I awoke at 3 a.m.. The noises were so terrible that I felt I couldn't take anymore and rose with the intention of trying to 'end it all.' Stepping out of bed, I noticed the little bottle of Rescue Remedy that I keep on my bedside table for emergencies. Unbelievable as this may sound, I took three small sips from the bottle, and in less than a minute my panic had subsided, allowing me to fall asleep peacefully.

Stirling, Scotland

I get a powerful allergic reaction to a combination of pollution and cats. My eyes itch; I get a rash on the back of my knees and around my eyes; I sneeze; and, if I stay in that environment, I have coughing and retching spasms. The only thing that alleviates my distress is Rescue Remedy.

East Hampton, New York

During a bout of sinusitis with associated congestion and pain, I poured a diluted dose of Rescue Remedy in my palm and sniffed it up each nostril; it was not pleasant, but it was most effective. I patted the rest of the dose over my sinuses, and the relief was almost instantaneous. I have shared this knowledge with several other folks who also report excellent results.*

Christchurch, New Zealand

---

*Rescue Remedy cream can be used here in the same way.

I began to prepare for a difficult heart operation by taking the Rescue Remedy each day. I took it full strength right before the operation, a double-bypass and mitral valve replacement, and then again each hour afterwards in the intensive care unit.

Following my operation, I had an unusually rapid recovery. This surprised the doctors, who felt it would be at least six months before I could do much of anything. I continued to take the remedy and was back at work before three months were up. Even now, during my checkups, the doctors are amazed at how swift my recovery was.

United States

A friend of mine who is an accomplished runner took regular doses of Rescue Remedy while running a thirty-one-mile marathon. After his seven-and-a-half-hour run, he had no soreness or significant exhaustion; he said he felt better than he did after any previous run.

In another incident: A thirty-eight year-old acquaintance of mine who was not used to strenuous exercise took a three-hour hike over snow, ice, and rocks, while wearing only soft moccasins. After his walk he took a hot shower, then applied the Rescue Remedy cream to his calves and to the soles of his feet. Shortly thereafter, he reported happily that there was no muscle soreness or swelling in his feet or legs.

New Mexico

My lips were chapped to the point where I could not smile, eat, or talk. My lower lip was also split about one-eighth of an inch. I applied Rescue Remedy cream to my lips, and within minutes I felt a great deal of relief from the pain—I could even smile again. I applied the cream several times that day and the next, and on the third day, I found I didn't need it any more. The split had come together, and my lips had completely healed.

New York City, New York

Years ago, my fingernails began to crack, flake, peel and split, and I tried every sort of cream and nail-hardener on the market—calcium tablets, cod liver oil, iodine, biochemic remedies. All proved ineffective. Finally, I bought a set of false nails, which I wore on social occasions. Five weeks ago, as I was rubbing Rescue Remedy cream into a bad bruise on my hand, I absent-mindedly smoothed it on my nails and cuticles. It worked! Now I am showing everyone my really lovely, healthy, strong, long fingernails. I am absolutely thrilled.

Plymouth, England

One of my co-workers was in pain during her menstrual cycle. She was sitting with her head on her desk, almost fainting. I squeezed a few drops of Rescue Remedy into a glass of water and urged her to drink it. She did, and to her great surprise, the pain diminished, then stopped almost immediately. Afterwards, she was able to finish her day's work without a recurrence of the pains or cramps.

Berkshire, England

Not getting consistent results from the various steroid creams I had been taking, I followed the suggestion of a homoeopathic physician and used the Rescue Remedy cream for an irritating eczema on my arms. I applied it two or three times a day, and after several weeks, the area improved greatly. Since last year, there have been very few recurrences, and those few promptly disappear when I apply a little Rescue Remedy cream.

Los Angeles, California

Rescue Remedy helped my wife deal with her emotional stress throughout the most severe and fearsome period of continuous illness that she has ever had. I believe that Rescue Remedy, which she took frequently during this period, stabilized her to the point that she was able to cope with her situation in a way that saved her life.

Arizona

Animals: Professional and Consumer Use

Out of thousands of case studies, some of the most extraordinary and dramatic reports have been those involving the use of the Bach Flower Remedies and Rescue Remedy with animals. The following is a compilation of cases from veterinarians and other professionals working with animals, as well as from individual consumers and pet owners.

Many veterinarians, using the Rescue Remedy as a last resort after standard procedures had failed, reported remarkable results.

It should be noted however, that the cases outlined here represent the use of Rescue Remedy with animals; and is not meant to imply its use or effectiveness for similar situations or conditions in humans.

Although the exact way in which the Bach remedies and the Rescue Remedy work is not yet known, the many animal reports outlined here strongly indicate that the remedies are not placebos. In light of this, the importance of further controlled studies cannot be emphasized enough.

Animals: Professional Testimonies

"I strongly encourage all my fellow veterinarians to use Rescue Remedy. I have used it, especially with dogs, in cases of shock, accidents, injuries, presurgical work, and tooth extractions. It does make a difference in reducing anxiety and calming the animals down so they are less susceptible to stress. In addition, it generally makes the anaesthetic procedure go a lot smoother. I believe the Rescue Remedy affects the higher centers of the brain. Dr. Bach was a medical genius; he had tremendous insight in knowing which plant would affect particular conditions."

George MacLeod, DVSM, MRCVS, England;
one of the world's foremost authorities on
the use of homoeopathic remedies for animals;
president, British Association of Homoeopathic
Veterinary Surgeons;
author of four major books on the use of
homoeopathy with animals

"We have found the Bach Flower Remedies and especially Rescue Remedy very helpful in alleviating a wide range of problems and conditions affecting all types of birds and animals. In addition, I have found the Rescue Remedy cream invaluable for insect and animal bites. We regard animals as equal to humans and they deserve equal treatment. In our experience, we have found the Rescue Remedy and the other Bach remedies an invaluable healing tool we would not want to be without."

John Bryant, former manager,
Ferne Animal Sanctuary,
Chard, Somerset, England

"Rescue Remedy, especially combined with Arnica (a homoeopathic remedy), is helpful in various types of animal emergencies, such as shock. I would encourage other veterinarians to try it. I would also like to see more work in testing and assessing the [benefits of] Rescue Remedy, for it has a tremendous potential in veterinary medicine."

Christopher Day, MB, MRCVS,
Stanford-in-the-vale, England;
author of *Homoeopathic Treatment of Small
Animals* (London: Wigmore Publications Ltd, 1984)

In his book, *Dr. Pitcairn's Complete Guide to Natural Health for Dogs and Cats,* Dr. Pitcairn recommends Rescue Remedy, for animals, used along with cardiopulmonary resuscitation, acupressure, external heart-massage, and other modalities, for various conditions.

For information on Dr. Pitcairn's recommendations, consult his book's special guide to handling emergencies, pp. 259-266.

"I have used Rescue Remedy to treat injured birds, newborn puppies, and kittens that are very weak, often with excellent results. I also use Rescue Remedy after difficult surgery, and in many cases this will make a significant difference in the animal waking up more quickly and easily."

Richard H. Pitcairn, DVM, PhD,
Eugene, Oregon;
author of *Dr. Pitcairn's Complete
Guide to Natural Health for Dogs
and Cats* (Emmaus, Pennsylvania;
Rodale Press, 1982)

"I use Rescue Remedy especially with newborn animals after a Caesarean section. The remedy seems particularly effective in compensating for the depressing quality of anaesthesia produced in the progeny [offspring]. Further, I consider it an outstanding aid to the harmonious survival of the young animal's family, including an anxious sire."

J.L. Newns, BVetMed, MRCVS,
Cornwall, England

"I have found the Bach Flower Rescue Remedy extremely effective in postsurgical instances. It is extraordinary in reviving pups after Caesareans. I administer Rescue Remedy during the cleanup stage once the throat is cleared; I find this to be most effective in improving the puppies' respiration and in bringing [the animals] back to normal.

"I use and recommend Rescue Remedy in situations involving the collapse of any young animal. It's a means of buying time. It's an excellent adjunct to any other treatment used for and during an immediate crisis. Try it; don't be concerned with [why or] how it works, since you might deprive yourself of a wonderful healing tool."

J.G.C. Saxton, BVetMed, MRCVS,
Leeds, England

"I use the Bach Flower Remedies on dogs that are under stress and need to relax. I also use the remedies during acupuncture therapy. Ninety percent of the time I get good to excellent results; only ten percent of the cases show little or no effect. I have used Rescue Remedy with animals that have been hit by cars or are in shock after surgery. It really does make a difference. I think that everyone, especially veterinarians, should have Rescue Remedy on hand. It is so effective yet inexpensive that it would be senseless not to try it. If it helps to get the animal out of shock, or even to calm down, it's worth it."

John B. Limehouse, DVM,
North Hollywood, California

"The Bach Flower Remedies are one of the most humane and gentle systems of healing I know. During their development, no animals were required to be sacrificed to prove the remedies' efficacy. They are a tremendous gift of healing for animals. In addition, the Bach remedies can help a person tune in to [himself] and become more sensitive to the animals.

"The more we use the remedies ourselves, the more our understanding of animals' emotions become clear. Careful observation has shown that animals tend to develop the same problems their owners have, especially psychosomatic ones. In addition, animals often have to cope with loneliness, anxiety, and fear. Rescue Remedy is highly recommended for all crises, and especially before and after surgery. We have found, when the remedies are used as indicated, that animals tend to recover very, very quickly."

Rebecca Hall, London, England;
author of *Animals Are Equal:
An Exploration of Animal Consciousness*
(London: Wildwood House, 1983) and
Voiceless Victims (London: Wildwood House, 1984)

"As a veterinary surgeon in general practice, I regularly administer Rescue Remedy for cases involving birth trauma, accident trauma, and post-Caesarean section....

"Often following a difficult birth, puppies or kittens that have been a long time in the birth canal will be slow in taking up the challenge of life. Rescue Remedy dripped on their tongues will give them that impetus to survive.

"Many animals born by Caesarean section often suffer before birth from respiratory depression as a result of the anaesthetic reaching them via their mother's blood stream. Rescue Remedy appears to stimulate their respiration and assist them in eliminating the toxic effects.

"I have had encouraging results using the remedy with lambs that have experienced a difficult birth. This is especially common with small hill ewes. Very often the newborn are suffering from bruising, exhaustion, and shock; their mothers may also be in a similar condition. For both, Rescue Remedy can be a great aid to recovery.

"I also use Rescue Remedy as a standard treatment for wild and domestic birds...[when] the animals are in shock and exhausted: birds that have been attacked by cats or hit by cars; [birds that have] flown into windows, [or fallen] out of their nests; sea birds blown ashore following severe storms; and birds recovering from anaesthetics. In these cases, I will generally administer two to three drops of the Rescue Remedy into the throat, place the bird in a dark box by a heat source, and leave it for about two hours. Often this is the only treatment required. In other cases, it will have helped the bird to be able to cope with further handling and therapy.

"I would encourage all veterinarians to have Rescue Remedy on hand. This is not a miracle medicine, but used regularly where indicated, it has much to recommend it. Inevitably there will be a case, as I have experienced, where Rescue Remedy will have such a profound and startling effect during a crisis that it will leave little doubt as to its efficacy."

Bruce Borland, BVetMed, MRCVS,
Bearsden, Scotland

"I use Rescue Remedy as a routine part of my veterinary practice in pre- and postoperative surgery. In accidents, Rescue Remedy helps animals overcome the shock of strange surroundings and assists with a more rapid recovery. The Rescue Remedy can be administered orally, put in drinking water, or dropped directly on and in the mouth. One of the great benefits of using the Bach remedies, including Rescue Remedy, is that they will not interfere with any other medicine or treatment the animal may be involved in. I would never hesitate using any of the Bach remedies.

"In my experience I have also found that one or two drops of Rescue Remedy will have an almost immediate effect on regulating and deepening an animal's breathing on coming out of an anaesthetic.

"I would further recommend that zookeepers have and use all the Bach remedies, especially Rescue Remedy. Simplicity is the key with the Bach system. I would use them [the remedies] in conjunction with other methods without reservations."

Eileen Wheeler, MRCVS,
Wales, United Kingdom

"I keep both Rescue Remedy cream and liquid available at all times, as I find them an invaluable aid in my veterinary work. They even work on wounds that would usually be slow to heal, as is the case with tortoises. The cream keeps the wounds supple, relieves pain, and speeds up the healing process. As I work with several animal rescue organizations, I am often called upon to treat sick or injured wild creatures, including foxes, badgers, and deer. Rescue Remedy liquid assists greatly by allaying their fear and panic; it also helps them to regain consciousness after being caught in wire snares.

"Birds benefit also from the Rescue Remedy; my standard treatment is to give them Rescue Remedy mixed with honey, then immediately put them into an enclosed box, in a warm, quiet place. After only twenty minutes they are calmer, stronger, and [able to] be handled with less risk of their dying from shock. I have found Rescue Remedy liquid to be extremely effective with creatures suffering emotional traumas and various forms of neuroses....I notice a significant increase in the recovery and survival rates of the wild and domestic species that I have treated since I started using the Bach remedies several years ago."

Sue Smith, veterinary nurse,
Chard, England

Animals: Professional Use

"Not long ago a colleague reported a case of a thoroughbred horse that had gone through long, drawn-out surgery involving the exploration of a tumour in the perineum area. The horse was given Rescue Remedy for three days before, and again after, the operation. During subsequent checkups, the veterinarian was staggered that the animal had recovered so quickly from such a traumatic procedure."

Eileen Wheeler, MRCVS,
Wales, United Kingdom

"Recently while I was carrying out a routine operation on a young toy poodle, it suffered an acute anaesthetic crisis with both the respiration and the heart stopping. The dog was given heart massage, artificial respiration and cardiac stimulants, but to no avail. When all else had failed, I gave the animal a few drops of Rescue Remedy under the tongue. Twenty seconds later the dog took an enormous breath and the heart started pumping. With further doses of remedy, both pulse and respiration were stabilised, the surgery was completed and the dog made an uneventful recovery. My nurse witnessed all this and looked at the poodle with disbelief. This seems a classic case where everything was traditionally done, but Rescue Remedy used as a last resort, saved the day and the dog. I was extremely impressed and continue to use the remedy in my practice."

In another case: "A Labrador bitch was presented for surgery with a ruptured diaphragm, the result of a road traffic accident. This condition always constitutes an extra anaesthetic risk. Once the animal was anaesthetised and surgery was commenced, it suffered respiratory and cardiac arrest. The dog failed to respond to orthodox methods of resuscitation but did respond to a dose of Rescue Remedy . As with the poodle, the heart started beating again and breathing was established voluntarily.

"Even effective procedures do not work in every case and I have had many cases where Rescue Remedy has been of no help. However, I am convinced of its great value and always have it to hand."

Bruce Borland, BVetMed, MRCVS,
Bearsden, Scotland

"I have recently used Rescue Remedy with a bulldog that was having a mild seizure. He was in a state of panic and was having severe respiratory difficulty. I administered Rescue Remedy at half-hour intervals for three to four hours and found it to be more effective than any sedative I could have used."

J.G.C. Saxton, BVetMed, MRCVS,
Leeds, England

"I was visiting a veterinarian friend of mine when another friend brought in a cat that appeared to be quite exhausted. The cat had been out in the rain all day and appeared frightened. We gave it one dose of Rescue Remedy, and within five minutes it was purring, cozy, and friendly."

G.S. Khalsa, MD,
Lathrup Village, Michigan

"I had a case where a dog was quite nervous and the owners wanted to tranquillize him before going on a long trip. I suggested the Bach Rescue Remedy as often as needed. Upon their return, the owners enthusiastically rang back to say that the remedy had helped remarkably to calm the animal down."

P.A. Culpin, MRCVS,
Surrey, England

"Not long ago a dog was brought into my office after being hit by a car. He wasn't very active, his gums were gray, and the time it took for his capillaries to fill was very slow. He had been hit extremely hard, but had no concussion. I gave him two doses of Rescue Remedy fifteen minutes apart. Within a short time his capillary filling time improved, and he began to perk up and recover."

John B. Limehouse, DVM,
North Hollywood, California

"I have often found Rescue Remedy very helpful for my wild bird patients. I particularly remember the case of a jackdaw suffering from severe head injuries. It was blind in one eye, infected with lice and grapeworms, thin and frail, and almost unconscious. I gave it a few drops of the Rescue Remedy on a child's paint brush, then wrapped it in wool and placed it in an electrically heated hospital cage, which I left in the dark. Soon I was handling a 'live' bird, warm and supple, conscious and alert, which I was able to attend to properly and give food. I am convinced that without the Rescue Remedy, this bird would not have regained consciousness or the will to live. In time it made a complete recovery, and its sight was saved. After it was released, it and another jackdaw used the house like a hotel for weeks, dropping in for a meal, for shelter from the rain, or just to look around."

M. Davidson,
The Bird Hospital,
Helston, Cornwall, England

Animals: Consumer Use

In the middle of March we discovered a small copper butterfly just free from her cocoon. We took her indoors, and for a whole week she remained motionless on a vase of flowers. Several times each day I sat her on a drop of Rescue Remedy on my finger. At last she unfurled her proboscis and took a long draught from the drop.

The result was immediate and almost startling. From being almost lifeless, she fluttered strongly about the room, but since the weather was still cold we kept her indoors for two more days, feeding her on fresh hyacinths and Rescue Remedy. One sunny morning at the end of that time, we opened the window and watched her fly on strong wings to freedom.

USA

My friend's dog became very lethargic when its master died. He walked around for days with his head down. Half an hour after I put four drops of Rescue Remedy on his tongue, he perked up and looked quite different. My friend continued putting drops into his drinking water for a couple of days, since then the dog has completely become himself again.

Newton Corner, Massachusetts

I use Rescue Remedy for all minor injuries that my dog and

cat sustain or when I know the animals are emotionally upset for some reason. It is the only medicine my dog doesn't shy away from; he even licks it off me when I use it.

Kansas City, Missouri

A six-month-old cat was brought in with a fishhook lodged in the pad of its right front paw. The cat was frantic and extremely difficult to control. Rescue Remedy, given orally and applied to the affected paw, calmed the cat down somewhat. Repeated applications allowed us to cut its pad with a razor blade and extract the fishhook with tweezers. I wrapped the paw in gauze and kept it wet with Rescue Remedy. During the one-week convalescence, the cat remained calm and chewed very little at the wrapping. The paw healed remarkably well.

Burkittsville, Maryland

I have an eight-month-old Labrador retriever that had cracked paws. I applied Rescue Remedy cream three times a day for one week. Compared to their normal condition, the paws remained in bad shape. But when I took the dog to the vet, I discovered that the paw condition was a result of distemper. The vet said that she had never seen paws in such good shape in a dog with distemper and wanted to know what I had been applying to them.

Madison, Wisconsin

My six-year-old male cat had a chronic abscess problem. No sooner did one abscess heal than another developed. His hair was falling out, and his eyes began to look very wild. A doctor friend told me about Rescue Remedy. I gave Thomas two doses a day, four drops in his mouth plus four drops in his drinking water. In two days the sores had new granulation and were drying; his coat felt smoother, and he was much calmer. Now he has a very smooth new coat; he is back to his normal weight; all the abscess holes are completely healed, and Thomas has his own bottle of Rescue Remedy.

Alameda, California

The Rescue Remedy cream has proved invaluable in a number of instances. A few days ago, I came across a horse that had hurt itself on barbed wire and had not eaten for two days. Its wound was raw and seemed painful to the touch. I gave the owner a jar of Rescue Remedy and told her to apply it to the affected area at regular intervals. She called one hour later, telling me that the horse began to graze. Two days later, the wound healed over.

New Mexico

I have given the Rescue Remedy to injured wild birds that dash themselves against my windows. It seems to bring them to consciousness quickly, and they fly off.

The most amazing recovery, however, was with my cat. Cats in this valley frequently get an intestinal disorder from which they eventually die. We imagine it comes from the field mice they eat. When my kitten developed the trouble, I thought of the Rescue Remedy. I administered the remedy for three consecutive mornings and nights, after which he recovered. A month later, the cat got sick again; I repeated the same treatment, and within a much shorter time he was better. Now eighteen months old, he eats mice and never seems to get sick. I've treated three of my neighbor's cats and got the same permanent results.

Yarrow, British Columbia

Oscar used to be a real fraidy cat, frightened of everything, including his own shadow. He was covered in eczema from head to tail, and we were always taking him to the vet. Six months ago, I decided to put him on the Bach remedies. I gave him the Rescue Remedy plus two other Bach remedies for his great fears. After administering three drops twice a day for nearly a week Oscar has become a changed animal. His eczema has cleared up, and he continues to be braver each week. Also, he has become extremely affectionate.

London, England

One of our Australian shepherds was running in the snow

and stepped on a broken bottle, cutting his foot. After cleaning it thoroughly and washing it in a herbal infusion, we coated the foot with Rescue Remedy cream and wrapped it. We gave the dog Rescue Remedy drops regularly and continued to coat the wound with the salve. We also dropped some of the remedy on his tongue before changing the bandage, and it always calmed him so that he didn't pull his leg away. After less than a week, his foot had completely healed without complications.

Colorado Springs, Colorado

One of my cats came bounding into the house with what looked like a dead baby chipmunk in its mouth. I pried the cat's jaws open, and the chipmunk hit the carpet with a thud. With no real hope of reviving it, I squirted some drops of Rescue Remedy into its mouth, and immediately it began to twitch and move around. It recovered so quickly that I barely had enough time to find a box for it. Fifteen minutes later, it was well enough for me to release it into the woods. Identical incidents occurred twice more during the next two months, one with a field mouse and another with a second chipmunk. Both animals revived after a dose of Rescue Remedy and were released in good health.

Ballston Lake, New York

We found a pregnant wallaby that was hit by a car on a country road. Her tiny, fully furred baby emerged. It was wriggling, struggling, and frantic. We decided to feed it, through an eyedropper, watered-down dried milk and raw sugar. The baby took the first few drops, but as the day drew on he seemed reluctant to take more. The tiny frame became skeletal and his attitude listless and dependent. We feared we were losing him.

It was then we thought of putting four drops of Rescue Remedy in his milk. Whether it was the taste of brandy, Rescue Remedy is in a brandy base, or whether he was just plain hungry, he took it until we were feeding him regularly.

Fortunately, the veterinary office was open the next day, and we took the wallaby by to show him to the vet. The doctor seemed quite surprised at the apparent health and comfort of our little friend and recommended that we continue our treatment.

For the next few days, we included the Rescue Remedy in his mixture. Today we can happily say that we have one healthy, bouncy, and bigger wallaby with us now.

Australia

We have had some marvelous experiences with the Rescue Remedy on animals. Our little Chihuahua once had a bad fall and became ill although the vet could find nothing wrong. The first dose of Rescue Remedy made a tremendous difference—the dog perked up amazingly. It was also a great help when she gave birth to her puppies. I don't know how I could manage without it.

California

Balludur was a twelve-month-old pedigree golden Labrador that completely distrusted people. No one had ever been able to touch him. Several times in a confined space he had lunged at people and bitten them.

This last time I'd gotten the idea of wetting a piece of bread with Rescue Remedy from the bottle I always carry. I did, and threw the dog a bit of the bread, which he ate. Ten minutes later, finding him still there, I wetted some more bread with the Rescue Remedy and squatted on my heels. To my amazement, he came and snatched it from my fingers and ran away. The following day, I fed him several bits by hand, and he let me rub his ears for a second before jumping away. From then on, he fed out of my hand like a normal dog and let me pat him, pull his tail, or put my hand in his mouth.

In three weeks he was behaving quite normally, contentedly stopping to sniff a trouser leg or to accept a pat or a bit of bread.

Farnborough, England

Our cat, Yarrow, caught a bird and was prevented from eating it just in time. The bird was unconscious, evidently suffering from shock. Frequent applications of the Rescue

Remedy to its head, eyes, beak, and feet helped so much that within fifteen minutes the bird was trying to fly. After another quarter of an hour, off it went.

Bermuda

I have used Rescue Remedy on one of my Lhasa Apsos that was terrified of thunder and lightning. She would panic and hyperventilate, run around looking for a place to hide, tremble, pant, and shake all over. About six months ago we began giving her a dose of Rescue Remedy as soon as she heard the first thunder. She's gotten to the point where she survives storms very well now. We don't have to keep treating her all the time. Last night we had a very bad storm, and the dog didn't bat an eyelash.

Down here we also have real flea epidemics, and my dogs get so irritated that they sometimes chew themselves incessantly. I've found that Rescue Remedy, given orally and put on the itchy spots, gives them relief. I use both the liquid and the cream. The remedy also calms them and cuts down on their frantic scratching.

St. Petersburg, Florida

We have a nine-year-old Chinese bantam chicken called Mrs., which had been trodden on by a horse. I carried Mrs. to her usual bed of hay and put Rescue Remedy around her beak and bathed her leg. I repeated this treatment frequently, until the little hen could drink water to which the Rescue Remedy and Bach remedy Crab Apple had been added.

After three days, one eye, which had closed, opened, and the chicken began to take a slight interest in tomato seeds and blackberries. I administered different Bach remedies according to her momentary moods, and her recovery is regarded as a real flower remedy miracle. She has no fear whatsoever of the ponies grazing around her now.

Godshill Ridge, England

A cat in my neighborhood was very lethargic and uncomfortable after delivering her kittens. She was barely eating and drinking, not good for a nursing mother. One night I gave her a dose of Rescue Remedy in her mouth and one during the next day. The following day, she was eating and drinking normally, happily nursing her kittens.

Albuquerque, New Mexico

Our eight-year-old Belgian shepherd, Fritz, had developed dysplasia, which hampered his ability to run and jump. After some time, his movements became more and more difficult. Our vet explained that Fritz's spinal nervous system was deteriorating and that a Vitamin C supplement might possibly improve the dog's condition. This formula worked for a period of time, but after awhile Fritz began to drag his paws, causing his toenails to be rubbed to the quick. He felt so much pain that eventually we had to carry him with a sling wrapped under his stomach. As a last resort, our vet prescribed steroids, but they had no effect.

Then one day a friend told us about Dr. Bach's Rescue Remedy. After obtaining the remedy, we put a few drops on Fritz's tongue, as our friend suggested. Fritz's first reaction was immediate; his eyes lit up, and his ears became erect.

Amazingly after some weeks of daily doses with the Rescue Remedy, Fritz's rear legs became more responsive, and he no longer needed the sling to help him. He stopped dragging his rear paws; his toenails grew back; and his spirit enlivened. Now, a year later, he walks with no difficulty.

The Dr. Bach Rescue Remedy has been a Godsend.

Chicago, Illinois

Recently, we had a bloated lamb that had reached the stage of lying on her side, gasping. She didn't have long to go when I thought of using the Rescue Remedy. I began administering it every few minutes for about an hour, when I was called away. When I returned about twenty minutes later, to my great surprise I found the lamb up and grazing as if nothing had ever happened. Since then we have saved many lambs suffering from bloat.

New South Wales, Australia

My kids were fishing off a pier when a bird fell into the water. They retrieved it and laid it down when our large dog grabbed it suddenly in his mouth. The children rescued the bird again and brought it to me. I could sense its shock and terror. I got two drops of Rescue Remedy into its beak twice before the day was over. The next day it seemed well, so we freed it, and it flew away.

DeSoto, Texas

I used to do foster work for the Great Dane Rescue League, taking in Great Danes that people could not keep. One day I took in a nine-month-old female Dane that had been living with a psychotic woman. The dog was the jumpiest, most neurotic creature I'd ever seen. For the first eight hours I couldn't get near her at all. It occurred to me to put Rescue Remedy into her drinking water, and after a day she calmed down quite a bit. I continued to treat her food and water for some weeks. Having become much more calm and stable, she was shortly thereafter adopted into a good home. I believe Rescue Remedy was the only thing that prevented her from being put to sleep.

Miami, Florida

My tortoise-shell cat, Tina, who is semi-wild, appeared one day with an enormous sheep tick behind her ear. I dropped some Rescue Remedy onto the tick's body two or three times, in addition to adding some to Tina's milk. In three days, the unpleasant parasite completely disappeared! It seemed to shrink in size and then one day just wasn't there. Evidently, ticks cannot withstand the high vibrations of the remedies.

Hampshire, England

My wife was in a hurry when she changed the water in our small goldfish bowl, adding the wrong water temperature. The fish went into shock. They were lying on their sides near the top of the bowl, apparently near death, with only sporadic movement of their gills. We put several drops of Rescue Remedy in the water, and within an hour the fish had completely recovered. The woman who handles goldfish at the pet shop assures me that it is almost unheard of for goldfish to survive the state of shock I described.

Texas

My four-year-old dog had a swollen eye and showed symptoms of allergies such as restlessness, panting, and difficult breathing. I applied several drops of diluted Rescue Remedy over her eyelid, on the tip of her nose, and in her mouth. Within a half-hour the respiratory symptoms and restlessness had abated, although the dog's eye was still swollen. Soon she became relaxed and sleepy, and after two or three more applications around the eye the swelling disappeared entirely.

Albuquerque, New Mexico

My horse's knee became swollen, and he couldn't put any of his weight on it. I rubbed some Rescue cream on it, and within fifteen minutes the horse was able to walk with a light limp. I rubbed more cream on his knee two or three times during the day. By the next day, there was no noticeable limp or swelling.

Albuquerque, New Mexico

Plants

In addition to humans and animals, the Bach Flower Remedies, as well as Rescue Remedy, are reported to be beneficial used on plants.

Plants are often affected by environmental and systemic weakness much in the same way that humans and animals are. For example, uprooting a plant without taking special precautions may result in shock, in which case the Rescue Remedy or the Bach remedy Star of Bethlehem could be helpful. Exhausted or drooping plants may be helped with either the Bach remedy Olive or Hornbeam. Infested or diseased plants may be helped, along with other appropriate treatments, by the Bach remedy Crab Apple. Other remedies may also be chosen, when a plant is 'out of sorts', by careful observation of plant behaviour and 'personality.' For example, a large overbearing plant which might give the impression of taking over the environment, may require the Bach remedy Vine; while a small delicate plant which seems to 'tremble' around people or things, may require the Bach remedy Aspen or Mimulus.

While dusting, I carelessly dropped one of our African violets face down. Sometime later it stopped drinking, its flowers fell off, and its leaves became limp. I thought it had died of shock, and I felt terrible! Shortly after this I decided to give it the Bach Rescue Remedy. In the beginning just a couple of drops at a time seemed to have a beneficial effect, though it did take a month for the plant to revive completely.

Bexhill-on-Sea, England

We had a cypress bush that was badly attacked by frost early this year. We gave it the Rescue Remedy every morning for about two weeks, and it really took a new lease on life. It is quite a happy and healthy bush now.

Manchester, England

So far, I have found several uses for Rescue Remedy in my garden. I am usually bothered with black slugs, especially on my radishes, but this year I sprinkled Rescue Remedy directly on my seeds before I covered them with earth, and I have had almost no slug activity since.

For all transplants, I put a few drops of Rescue Remedy on the roots before putting them into the ground, and then I give them a solution of five liters of water plus eight drops of Rescue Remedy. The transplants always do well after that.

This spring I've had to be away from the garden, sometimes for a week at a time. Often on my return I would find my flowers drooping quite a bit; however, I've found that if I water them that night with a solution of Rescue Remedy, they'd be bright and lovely in the morning.

Amsterdam, Holland

Our anemones were drooping and limp, looking as though they were about to die. We gave them Rescue Remedy, and within three hours they were perky; their stems had stiffened, and they looked jolly and bright.

Acton, England

One of my favourite miniature rhododendrons succumbed to the drought while we were on holiday. Completely leafless and brittle, it seemed a hopeless case. I applied the Rescue Remedy liquid to one-half of the bush. The treated section is now covered with glossy green leaves and flower buds, while the untreated section is completely dead.

Scotland

When we returned from vacation, I discovered that our favorite sansevieria had been traumatized during our absence. Left on a windowsill overnight, it had become chilled when the temperature dropped to twenty degrees. Its leaves were wrinkled and curled tight. We tried everything to revive it, but nothing worked until we watered and washed its leaves with a solution of spring water and Rescue Remedy. The next morning it started to open, and ten days later it was alive and healthy. It is doing fine now, thanks to Rescue Remedy.

Colorado Springs, Colorado

We had a young persimmon tree that was blown down by the wind and was almost completely severed to about one foot above the ground; only one thin thread of bark joined the two sections.

Without much optimism we placed the tree in an upright position, dressed the wound with bandages soaked in a solution of Rescue Remedy, and strapped the two sections tightly between wooden splints.

I kept the dressings moist with the medicine for several days, also watering the roots freely with a weak solution. Now, after this long, severe winter, our little tree is budding normally and shows no signs of the injury at all.

England

Conclusion

The reader may by now have gathered from the preceding pages that the healing effects of the Bach Flower Rescue Remedy on people, plants and animals seem remarkable, if not miraculous. The Rescue Remedy appears to work uniquely on each individual in moments of crisis, giving, for example, soothing relief from the sting of a bee, or quietness to the mind in a time of grief.

It is not the purpose of this work to claim phenomenal cures for serious conditions requiring professional treatments; nor is it to state that the Rescue Remedy should replace standard orthodox medical practice. The intent of this book is to demonstrate that the Rescue Remedy has been consistently used in the past fifty years as an invaluable healing adjunct, which is safe and has no reported side effects.

It has been shown that if standard treatment or first aid measures are not available, Rescue Remedy can make a critical difference in the recovery of the patient, especially by alleviating stressful states of mind. Case histories show that the Rescue Remedy may calm the individual and ease terror, anxiety, and fear involved with illness or injury, thereby helping the person to withstand the trauma while professional help is summoned. Even when treatment is immediately available, Rescue Remedy will augment that therapy by providing a feeling of comfort and safety. Reports indicate that psychotherapists and other health care professionals have found Bach Flower Remedies invaluable for calming anxiety or tension. As well as providing emotional comfort, the Rescue Remedy speeds the healing of physical injuries such as cuts, sprains, bruises, and other physical traumas in people, animals, and even plants.

The Rescue Remedy and Bach Flower Remedies should not be considered as drugs or addictive crutches, but as catalysts that bring about a balance in the individual's emotional and mental levels. The remedies enable some people to become more aware of their inner nature, often bringing insight which helps prevent future recurrence of problems or illness.

In today's society, lack of professional accessibility, high costs, ineffective cures, and undesirable side effects from drugs are some of the many factors contributing to a phenomenal rise of interest in medical self-care. As an indicator of this growing awareness, a report prepared by the Commission on Alternative Medicine in the Netherlands stated that the right of the individual to use an alternative/complementary medicine should be respected. Along similar lines in the United States, Joe Graedon, the Drugs Editor of "Medical Self-Care", and the author of *The People's Pharmacy* and *The People's Pharmacy II*, stated that ". . . if the remedy is harmless and inexpensive and the possible rewards are great, you may decide to conduct your own experiment without waiting for the double-blind studies. Part of self-care is being aware of the no-man's land where some pretty respectable experts say therapy 'x' works, but the final verdict isn't in . . . the final decision is yours."

To date, Rescue Remedy has not had any clinical trials. However, it is anticipated that research work will be carried out using clinical studies to prove the healing effects of the Rescue Remedy and other Bach Flower Remedies. In the interim, the testimonials included in this book from the many scientifically trained medical practitioners may serve to answer any queries concerning the Rescue Remedy's safety and effectiveness. Although some critics may consider these testimonials to be subjective reporting, it should be pointed out that the history of pharmacy is full of examples where folk medicines were subsequently validated.

The case histories reported earlier were based on the use of the Rescue Remedy that is produced by the Bach Centre in Great Britain. As with many successful quality products, there are often imitations which follow and the Bach Flower Remedies are no exception.

A month before he died, Dr. Edward Bach wrote a letter to Victor Bullen, his assistant, on 26 October 1936, foretelling that there would be others who would want to change, add to, and delete from his system of healing. He wrote:

Dear Vic,

I think now you have seen every phase of this Work.

This last episode of Doctor Max Wolf may be welcomed. It is a proof of the value of our Work when material agencies arise to distort it, because the distortion is a far greater weapon than attempted destruction.

Mankind asked for free-will, which God granted him, hence mankind must always have a choice.

As soon as a teacher has given his work to the world, a contorted version of the same must arise.

Such has happened even from the humblest like ourselves, who have dedicated our services to the good of our fellow-men, even to the Highest of all, the Divinity of Christ.

The contortion must be raised for people to be able to choose between the gold and the dross.

Our work is steadfastly to adhere to the simplicity and purity of this method of healing; and when the next edition of the *Twelve Healers* becomes necessary, we must have a longer introduction, firmly upholding the harmlessness, the simplicity and the miraculous healing powers of the Remedies, which have been shown to us through a greater Source than our own intellects.

I feel now, dear Brother, that as I find it more and more necessary to go into temporary solitude, you have the whole situation in hand and can cope with all matters either connected with patients or connected with the administration of this work of healing, knowing that people like ourselves who have tested the glory of self-sacrifice, the glory of helping our brothers, once we have been given a jewel of such magnitude, nothing can deviate us from our path of love and duty to displaying its lustre, pure and unadorned, to the people of the world.

Since then, many "people of the world" continue to benefit from his gentle system of healing.

Without Dr. Bach's deep insight into and understanding of the nature of disease, his gentle system of healing would not have evolved.

As nothing can replace Edward Bach's original writings, *Ye Suffer From Yourselves* and *Free Thyself* are provided for the reader's reflection and upliftment.

APPENDIX A

Ye Suffer
From Yourselves

by
EDWARD BACH
M.B., B.S., M.R.C.S., L.R.C.P., D.P.H.

An Address given at Southport, February, 1931.

IN coming to address you this evening, I find the task not an easy one.

You are a medical society, and I come to you as a medical man: yet the medicine of which one would speak is so far removed from the orthodox views of today, that there will be little in this paper which savours of the consulting room, nursing home, or hospital ward as we know them at present.

Were it not that you, as followers of Hahnemann, are already vastly in advance of those who preach the teachings of Galen, and the orthodox medicine of the last two thousand years, one would fear to speak at all.

But the teaching of your great Master and his followers has shed so much light upon the nature of disease, and opened up so much of the road which leads to correct healing, that I know you will be prepared to come with me further along that path, and see more of the glories of perfect health, and the true nature of disease and cure.

The inspiration given to Hahnemann brought a light to humanity in the darkness of materialism, when man had come to consider disease as a purely materialistic problem to be relieved and cured by materialistic means alone.

He, like Paracelsus, knew that if your spiritual and mental aspects were in harmony, illness could not exist: and he set out to find remedies which would treat our minds, and thus bring us peace and health.

Hahnemann made a great advance and carried us a long way along the road, but he had only the length of one life in which to work, and it is for us to continue his researches where he left off: to add more to the structure of perfect healing of which he laid the foundation, and so worthily began the building.

The homoeopath has already dispensed with much of the unnecessary and unimportant aspects of orthodox medicine, but he has yet further to go. I know that you wish to look forward, for neither the knowledge of the past nor the present is sufficient for the seeker after truth.

Paracelsus and Hahnemann taught us not to pay too much attention to the details of disease, but to treat the personality, the inner man, realising that if our spiritual and mental natures were in harmony disease disappeared. That great foundation to their edifice is the fundamental teaching which must continue.

Hahnemann next saw how to bring about this harmony, and he found that among the drugs and the remedies of the old school, and among elements and plants which he himself selected, he could reverse their action by potentisation, so that the same substance which gave rise to poisonings and symptoms of disease, could — in the minutest quantity — cure those particular symptoms when prepared by his special method.

Thus formulated he the law of "like cures like": another great fundamental principle of life. And he left us to continue the building of the temple, the earlier plans of which had been disclosed to him.

And if we follow on this line of thought, the first great

realisation which comes upon us is the truth that it is disease itself which is "like curing like": because disease is the result of wrong activity. It is the natural consequence of disharmony between our bodies and our Souls: it is "like curing like" because it is the very disease itself which hinders and prevents our carrying our wrong actions too far, and at the same time, is a lesson to teach us to correct our ways, and harmonise our lives with the dictates of our Soul.

Disease is the result of wrong thinking and wrong doing, and ceases when the act and thought are put in order. When the lesson of pain and suffering and distress is learnt, there is no further purpose in its presence, and it automatically disappears.

This is what Hahnemann incompletely saw as "like curing like."

COME A LITTLE FURTHER ALONG THE ROAD.

Another glorious view then opens out before us, and here we see that true healing can be obtained, not by wrong repelling wrong, but by right replacing wrong: good replacing evil: light replacing darkness.

Here we come to the understanding that we no longer fight disease with disease: no longer oppose illness with the products of illness: no longer attempt to drive out maladies with such substances that can cause them: but, on the contrary, to bring down the opposing virtue which will eliminate the fault.

And the pharmacopoeia of the near future should contain only those remedies which have the power to bring down good, eliminating all those whose only quality is to resist evil.

True, hate may be conquered by a greater hate, but it can only be cured by love: cruelty may be prevented by a greater cruelty, but only eliminated when the qualities of sympathy and pity have developed: one fear may be lost and forgotten in the presence of a greater fear, but the real cure of all fear is perfect courage.

And so now, we of this school of medicine have to turn our attention to those beautiful remedies which have been Divinely placed in nature for our healing, amongst those beneficent, exquisite plants and herbs of the countryside.

It is obviously fundamentally wrong to say that "like cures like." Hahnemann had a conception of the truth right enough, but expressed it incompletely. Like may strengthen like, like may repel like, but in the true healing sense like cannot cure like.

If you listen to the teachings of Krishna, Buddha, or Christ, you will find always the teachings of good overcoming evil. Christ taught us not to resist evil, to love our enemies, to bless those who persecute us — there is no like curing like in this. And so in true healing, and so in spiritual advancement, we must always seek good to drive out evil, love to conquer hate, and light to dispel darkness. Thus must we avoid all poisons, all harmful things, and use only the beneficent and beautiful.

No doubt Hahnemann, by his method of potentisation, endeavoured to turn wrong into right, poisons into virtues, but it is simpler to use the beauteous and virtuous remedies direct.

Healing, being above all materialistic things, and materialistic laws, Divine in its origin, is not bound by any of our conventions or ordinary standards. In this we have to raise our ideals, our thoughts, our aspirations, to those glorious and lofty realms taught and shown to us by the Great Masters.

Do not think for one moment that one is detracting from Hahnemann's work, on the contrary, he pointed out the great fundamental laws, the basis; but he had only one life: and had he continued his work longer, no doubt he would have progressed along these lines. We are merely advancing his work, and carrying it to the next natural stage.

Let us now consider why medicine must so inevitably change. The science of the last two thousand years has regarded disease as a material factor which can be eliminated by material means: such, of course, is entirely wrong.

Disease of the body, as we know it, is a result, an end product, a final stage of something much deeper. Disease originates above the physical plane, nearer to the mental. It is entirely the result of a conflict between our spiritual and mortal selves. So long as these two are in harmony, we are in perfect health: but when there is discord, there follows what we know as disease.

Disease is solely and purely corrective: it is neither vindictive nor cruel: but it is the means adopted by our own Souls to point out to us our faults: to prevent our making greater errors: to hinder us from doing more harm: and to bring us back to that path of Truth and Light from which we should never have strayed.

Disease is, in reality, for our good, and is beneficent, though we should avoid it if we had but the correct understanding, combined with the desire to do right.

Whatever error we make, it reacts upon ourselves, causing us unhappiness, discomfort, or suffering, according to its nature. The object being to teach us the harmful effect of wrong action or thought: and, by its producing similar results upon ourselves, shows us how it causes distress to others, and is hence contrary to the Great and Divine Law of Love and Unity.

To the understanding physician, the disease itself points out the nature of the conflict. Perhaps this is best illustrated by giving you examples to bring home to you that no matter from what disease you may suffer, it is because there is disharmony between yourself and the Divinity within you, and that you are committing some fault, some error, which your Higher Self is attempting to correct.

Pain is the result of cruelty which causes pain to others, and may be mental or physical: but be sure that if you suffer pain, if you will but search yourselves you will find that some hard action or hard thought is present in your nature: remove this, and your pain will cease. If you suffer from stiffness of joint or limb, you can be equally certain that there is stiffness in your mind; that you are rigidly holding on to some idea, some principle, some convention may be, which you should not have. If you suffer from asthma, or difficulty in breathing, you are in some way stifling another personality; or from lack of courage to do right, smothering yourself. If you waste, it is because you are allowing someone to obstruct your own life-force from entering your body. Even the part of the body affected indicates the nature of the fault. The hand, failure or wrong in action: the foot, failure to assist others: the brain, lack of control: the heart, deficiency or excess, or wrong doing in the aspect of love: the eye, failure to see aright and comprehend the truth when placed before you. And so, exactly, may be worked out the reason and nature of an infirmity: the lesson required of the patient: and the necessary correction to be made.

Let us now glance, for a moment, at the hospital of the future.

It will be a sanctuary of peace, hope, and joy. No hurry: no noise: entirely devoid of all the terrifying apparatus and appliances of today: free from the smell of antiseptics and anaesthetics: devoid of everything that suggests illness and suffering. There will be no frequent taking of temperatures to disturb the patient's rest: no daily examinations with stethoscopes and tappings to impress upon the patient's mind the nature of his illness. No constant feeling of the pulse to suggest that the heart is beating too rapidly. For all these things remove the very atmosphere of peace and calm that is so necessary for the patient to bring about his speedy recovery. Neither will there be any need for laboratories; for the minute and microscopic examination of detail will no longer matter when it is fully realised that it is the patient to be treated and not the disease.

The object of all institutions will be to have an atmosphere of peace, and of hope, of joy, and of faith. Everything will be done to encourage the patient to forget his illness; to strive for health; and at the same time to correct any fault in his nature; and come to an understanding of the lesson which he has to learn.

Everything about the hospital of the future will be uplifting and beautiful, so that the patient will seek that refuge, not only to be relieved of his malady, but also to develop the desire to live a life more in harmony with the dictates of his Soul than had been previously done.

The hospital will be the mother of the sick; will take them up in her arms; soothe and comfort them; and bring them hope, faith and courage to overcome their difficulties.

The physician of tomorrow will realise that he of himself has no power to heal, but that if he dedicates his life to the service of his brother-men; to study human nature so that he may, in part, comprehend its meaning; to desire whole-heartedly to relieve suffering, and to surrender all for the help of the sick; then, through him may be sent knowledge to guide them, and the power of healing to relieve their pain. And even then, his power and ability to help will be in proportion to his intensity of desire and his willingness to serve. He will understand that health, like life, is of God, and God alone. That he and the remedies that he uses are merely instruments and agents in the Divine Plan to assist to bring the sufferer back to the path of the Divine Law.

He will have no interest in pathology or morbid anatomy; for his study will be that of health. It will not matter to him whether, for example, shortness of breath is caused by the tubercle baccillus, the streptococcus, or any other organism: but it will matter intensely to know why the patient should have to suffer difficulty of breathing. It will be of no moment to know which of the valves of the heart is damaged, but it will be vital to realise in what way the patient is wrongly developing his love aspect. X-rays will no longer be called into use to examine an arthritic joint, but rather research into the patient's mentality to discover the stiffness in his mind.

The prognosis of disease will no longer depend on physical signs and symptoms, but on the ability of the patient to correct his fault and harmonise himself with his Spiritual Life.

The education of the physician will be a deep study of human nature; a great realisation of the pure and perfect: and an understanding of the Divine state of man: and the knowledge of how to assist those who suffer that they may harmonise their conduct with their Spiritual Self, so that they may bring concord and health to the personality.

He will have to be able, from the life and history of the patient, to understand the conflict which is causing disease or disharmony between the body and Soul, and thus enable him to give the necessary advice and treatment for the relief of the sufferer.

He will also have to study Nature and Nature's Laws: be conversant with Her Healing Powers, that he may utilise these for the benefit and advantage of the patient.

The treatment of tomorrow will be essentially to bring four qualities to the patient.

First, peace: secondly, hope: thirdly, joy: and fourthly, faith.

And all the surroundings and attention will be to that end.

To surround the patient with such an atmosphere of health and light as will encourage recovery. At the same time, the errors of the patient, having been diagnosed, will be pointed out, and assistance and encouragement given that they may be conquered.

In addition to this, those beautiful remedies, which have been Divinely enriched with healing powers, will be administered, to open up those channels to admit more of the light of the Soul, that the patient may be flooded with healing virtue.

The action of these remedies is to raise our vibrations and open up our channels for the reception of our Spiritual Self, to flood our natures with the particular virtue we need, and wash out from us the fault which is causing harm. They are able, like beautiful music, or any gloriously uplifting thing which gives us inspiration, to raise our very natures, and bring us nearer to our Souls: and by that very act, to bring us peace, and relieve our sufferings.

They cure, not by attacking disease, but by flooding our bodies with the beautiful vibrations of our Higher Nature, in the presence of which disease melts as snow in the sunshine.

And, finally, how they must change the attitude of the patient towards disease and health.

Gone forever must be the thought that relief may be obtained by the payment of gold or silver. Health, like life, is of Divine origin, and can only be obtained by Divine Means. Money, luxury, travel, may outwardly appear to be able to purchase for us an improvement in our physical being: but these things can never give us true health.

The patient of tomorrow must understand that he, and he alone, can bring himself relief from suffering, though he may obtain advice and help from an elder brother who will assist him in his effort.

Health exists when there is perfect harmony between Soul and mind and body: and this harmony, and this harmony alone, must be attained before cure can be accomplished.

In the future there will be no pride in being ill: on the contrary, people will be as ashamed of sickness as they should be of crime.

And now I want to explain to you two conditions which are probably giving rise to more disease in this country than any other single cause: the great failings of our civilisation — greed and idolatory.

Disease, is, of course, sent to us as a correction. We bring it entirely upon ourselves: it is the result of our own wrong doing and wrong thinking. Can we but correct our faults and live in harmony with the Divine Plan, illness can never assail us.

In this, our civilisation, greed overshadows all. There is greed for wealth, for rank, for position, for worldly honours, for comfort, for popularity: yet it is not of these one would speak, because even they are, in comparison, harmless.

The worst of all is the greed to possess another individual. True, this is so common amongst us that it has come to be looked upon as almost right and proper: yet that does not mitigate the evil: for, to desire possession or influence over another individual or personality, is to usurp the power of our Creator.

How many folk can you number amongst your friends or relations who are free? How many are there who are not bound or influenced or controlled by some other human being? How many are there who could say, that day by day, month by month, and year by year, "I obey only the dictates of my Soul, unmoved by the influence of other people?"

And yet, everyone of us is a free Soul, answerable only to God for our actions, aye, even our very thoughts.

Possibly the greatest lesson of life is to learn freedom. Freedom from circumstances, environment, other personalities, and most of all from ourselves: because until we are free we are unable fully to give and to serve our brother-men.

Remember that whether we suffer disease or hardship: whether we are surrounded by relations or friends who may annoy us: whether we have to live amongst those who rule and dictate to us, who interfere with our plans and hamper our progress, it is of our own making: it is because there is still within us a trace left to bar the freedom of someone: or the absence of courage to claim our own individuality, our birthright.

The moment that we ourselves have given complete liberty to all around us: when we no longer desire to bind and limit: when we no longer expect anything from anyone: when our only thought is to give and give and never to take, that moment shall we find that we are free of all the world: our bonds will fall from us: our chains be broken: and for the first time in our lives shall we know the exquisite joy of perfect liberty. Freed from all human restraint, the willing and joyous servant of our Higher Self alone.

So greatly has the possessive power developed in the West that it is necessitating great disease before people will recognise the error and correct their ways: and according to the severity and type of or domination over another, so must we suffer as long as we continue to usurp a power which does not belong to man.

Absolute freedom is our birthright, and this we can only obtain when we grant that liberty to every living Soul who may come into our lives. For truly we reap as we sow, and truly "as we mete so it shall be measured out to us."

Exactly as we thwart another life, be it young or old, so must that react upon ourselves. If we limit their activities, we may find our bodies limited with stiffness: if, in addition, we cause them pain and suffering, we must be prepared to bear the same, until we have made amends: and there is no disease, even however severe, that may not be needed to check our actions and alter our ways.

To those of you who suffer at the hands of another, take courage; for it means that you have reached that stage of advancement when you are being taught to gain your freedom: and the very pain and suffering which you are bearing is teaching you how to correct your own fault, and as soon as you have realised the fault and put that right, your troubles are over.

The way to set about to do this work is to practise exquisite gentleness: never by thought or word or deed to hurt another. Remember that all people are working out their own salvation; are going through life to learn those lessons for the perfection of their own Soul; and that they must do it for themselves: that they must gain their own experiences: learn the pitfalls of the world, and, of their own effort, find the pathway which leads to the mountain top. The most that we can do is, when we have a little more knowledge and experience than a younger brother, very gently to guide them. If they will listen, well and good: if not, we must patiently wait until they have had further experience to teach them their fault, and then they may come to us again.

We should strive to be so gentle, so quiet, so patiently helpful that we move among our fellow men more as a breath of air or a ray of sunshine: ever ready to help them when they ask: but never forcing them to our own views.

And I want now to tell you of another great hindrance to health, which is very, very common today, and one of the greatest obstacles that physicians encounter in their endeavour to heal. An obstacle which is a form of idolatory. Christ said "Ye cannot serve God and mammon," and yet the service of mammon is one of our greatest stumbling blocks.

There was an angel once, a glorious, magnificent angel, that appeared to St. John, and St. John fell in adoration and worshipped. But the Angel said to him, "See thou do it not, I am thy fellow servant and of thy brethren. Worship God." And yet today, tens of thousands of us worship not God, not even a mighty angel, but a fellow human being. I can assure you that one of the greatest difficulties which has to be overcome is a sufferer's worship of another mortal.

How common is the expression: "I must ask my father, my sister, my husband." What a tragedy. To think that a human Soul, developing his Divine evolution, should stop to ask permission of a fellow traveller. To whom does he imagine that he owes his origin, his being, his life — to a fellow-traveller or to his Creator?

We must understand that we are answerable for our actions, and for our thoughts to God, and to God alone. And that to be influenced, to obey the wishes, or consider the desires of another mortal is idolatory indeed. Its penalty is severe, it binds us with chains, it places us in prisons, it confines our very life; and so it should, and so we justly deserve, if we listen to the dictates of a human being, when our whole self should know but one command — that of our Creator, Who gave us our life and our understanding.

Be certain that the individual who considers above his duty his wife, his child, his father, or his friend, is an idolator, serving mammon and not God.

Remember the words of Christ, "Who is My mother, and who are My brethren," which imply that even all of us, small and insignificant as we may be, are here to serve our brother-men, humanity, the world at large, and never, for the briefest moment, to be under the dictates and commands of another human individual against those motives which we know to be our Soul's commands.

Be captains of your Souls, be masters of your fate (which means let yourselves be ruled and guided entirely, without let or hindrance from person or circumstance, by the Divinity within you), ever living in accordance with the laws of, and answerable only to the God Who gave you your life.

And yet, one more point to bring before your notice. Ever remember the injunction which Christ gave to His disciples, "Resist not evil." Sickness and wrong are not to be conquered by direct fighting, but by replacing them by good. Darkness is removed by light, not by greater darkness: hate by love: cruelty by sympathy and pity: and disease by health.

Our whole object is to realise our faults, and endeavour so to develop the opposing virtue that the fault will disappear from us like snow melts in the sunshine. Don't fight your worries: don't struggle with your disease: don't grapple with your infirmities: rather forget them in concentrating on the development of the virtue you require.

And so now, in summing up, we can see the mighty part that homoeopathy is going to play in the conquest of disease in the future.

Now that we have come to the understanding that disease itself is "like curing like": that it is of our own making: for our correction and for our ultimate good: and that we can avoid it, if we will but learn the lessons needed, and correct our faults before the severer lesson of suffering is necessary. This is the natural continuation of Hahnemann's great work; the sequence of that line of thought which was disclosed to him, leading us a step further towards perfect understanding of disease and health, and is the stage to bridge the gap between where he left us and the dawn of that day when humanity will have reached that state of advancement when it can receive direct the glory of Divine Healing.

The understanding physician, selecting well his remedies from the beneficent plants in nature, those Divinely enriched and blessed, will be enabled to assist his patients to open up those channels which allow greater communion between Soul and body, and thus the development of the virtues needed to wipe away the faults. This brings to mankind the hope of real health combined with mental and spiritual advance.

For the patients, it will be necessary that they are prepared to face the truth, that disease is entirely and only due to faults within themselves, just as the wages of sin is death. They will have to have the desire to correct those faults, to live a better and more useful life, and to realise that healing depends on their own effort, though they may go to the physician for guidance and assistance in their trouble.

Health can be no more obtained by payment of gold than a child can purchase his education: no sum of money can teach the pupil to write, he must learn of himself, guided by an experienced teacher. And so it is with health.

There are the two great commandments: "Love God and thy neighbour." Let us develop our individuality that we may obtain complete freedom to serve the Divinity within ourselves, and that Divinity alone: and give unto all others their absolute freedom, and serve them as much as lies within our power, according to the dictates of our Souls, ever remembering that as our own liberty increases, so grows our freedom and ability to serve our fellow-men.

Thus we have to face the fact that disease is entirely of our own making, and that the only cure is to correct our faults. All true healing aims at assisting the patient to put his Soul and mind and body in harmony. This can only be done by himself, though advice and help by an expert brother may greatly assist him.

As Hahnemann laid down, all healing which is not from within, is harmful, and apparent cure of the body obtained through materialistic methods, obtained only through the action of others, without self-help, may certainly bring physical relief, but harm to our Higher Natures, for the lesson has remained unlearnt, and the fault has not been eradicated.

It is terrible today to think of the amount of artificial and superficial cures obtained through money and wrong methods in medicine; wrong methods because they merely suppress symptoms, give apparent relief, without removing the cause.

Healing must come from within ourselves, by acknowledging and correcting our faults, and harmonising our being with the Divine Plan. And as the Creator, in His mercy, has placed certain Divinely enriched herbs to assist us to our victory, let us seek out these and use them to be best of our ability, to help us climb the mountain of our evolution, until the day when we shall reach the summit of perfection.

Hahnemann had realised the truth of "like curing like," which is in reality disease curing wrong action: that true healing is one stage higher than this: love and all its attributes driving out wrong.

That in correct healing nothing must be used which relieves the patient of his own responsibility: but such means only must be adopted which help him to overcome his faults.

That we now know that certain remedies in the homoeopathic pharmacopoeia have the power to elevate our vibrations, thus bringing more union between our mortal and Spiritual self, and effecting the cure by greater harmony thus produced.

And finally, that it is our work to purify the pharmacopoeia, and to add to it new remedies until it contains only those which are beneficent and uplifting.

APPENDIX B

Free Thyself

by
EDWARD BACH
M.B., B.S., M.R.C.S., L.R.C.P., D.P.H.

INTRODUCTION

It is impossible to put truth into words. The author of this book has no desire to preach, indeed he very greatly dislikes that method of conveying knowledge. He has tried, in the following pages, to show as clearly and simply as possible the purpose of our lives, the uses of the difficulties that beset us, and the means by which we can regain our health; and, in fact, how each of us may become our own doctor.

Free Thyself

CHAPTER I.

It is as simple as this, the Story of Life.

A SMALL child has decided to paint the picture of a house in time for her mother's birthday. In her little mind the house is already painted; she knows what it is to be like down to the very smallest detail, there remains only to put it on paper.

Out comes the paint-box, the brush and the paint-rag, and full of enthusiasm and happiness she sets to work. Her whole attention and interest is centred on what she is doing — nothing can distract her from the work in hand.

The picture is finished in time for the birthday. To the very best of her ability she has put her idea of a house into form. It is a work of art because it is all her very own, every stroke done out of love for her mother, every window, every door painted in with the conviction that it is meant to be there. Even if it looks like a haystack, it is the most perfect house that has ever been painted: it is a success because the little artist has put her whole heart and soul, her whole being into the doing of it.

This is health, this is success and happiness and true service. Serving through love in perfect freedom in our own way.

So we come down into this world, knowing what picture we have to paint, having already mapped out our path through life, and all that remains for us to do is to put it into material form. We pass along full of joy and interest, concentrating all our attention upon the perfecting of that picture, and to the very best of our ability translating our own thoughts and aims into the physical life of whatever environment we have chosen.

Then, if we follow from start to finish our very own ideals, our very own desires with all the strength we possess, there is no failure, our life has been a tremendous success, a healthy and a happy one.

The same little story of the child-painter will illustrate how, if we allow them, the difficulties of life may interfere with this success and happiness and health, and deter us from our purpose.

The child is busily and happily painting when someone comes along and says, "Why not put a window here, and a door there; and of course the garden path should go this way." The result in the child will be complete loss of interest in the work; she may go on, but is now only putting someone else's ideas on paper: she may become cross, irritated, unhappy, afraid to refuse these suggestions; begin to hate the picture and perhaps tear it up: in fact, according to the type of child so will be the reaction.

The final picture may be a recognisable house, but it is an imperfect one and a failure because it is the interpretation of another's thoughts, not the child's. It is of no use as a birthday present because it may not be done in time, and the mother may have to wait another whole year for her gift.

This is disease, the reaction to interference. This is temporary failure and unhappiness: and this occurs when we allow others to interfere with our purpose in life, and implant in our minds doubt, or fear, or indifference.

CHAPTER II.

Health depends on being in harmony with our souls.

IT is of primary importance that the true meaning of health and of disease should be clearly understood.

Health is our heritage, our right. It is the complete and full union between soul, mind and body; and this is no difficult far-away ideal to attain, but one so easy and natural that many of us have overlooked it.

All earthly things are but the interpretation of things spiritual. The smallest most insignificant occurrence has a Divine purpose behind it.

We each have a Divine mission in this world, and our souls use our minds and bodies as instruments to do this work, so that when all three are working in unison the result is perfect health and perfect happiness.

A Divine mission means no sacrifice, no retiring from the world, no rejecting of the joys of beauty and nature; on the contrary, it means a fuller and greater enjoyment of all things: it means doing the work that we love to do with all our heart and soul, whether it be house-keeping, farming, painting, acting, or serving our fellow-men in shops or houses. And this work, whatever it may be, if we love it above all else, is the definite command of our soul, the work we have to do in this world, and in which alone we can be our true selves, interpreting in an ordinary materialistic way the message of that true self.

We can judge, therefore, by our health and by our happiness, how well we are interpreting this message.

There are all the spiritual attributes in the perfect man; and we come into this world to manifest these one at a time, to perfect and strengthen them so that no experience, no difficulty can weaken or deflect us from the fulfilment of this purpose. We chose the earthly occupation, and the external circumstances that will give us the best opportunities of testing us to the full: we come with the full realisation of our particular work: we come with the unthinkable privilege of knowing that all our battles are won before they are fought, that victory is certain before ever the test arrives, because we know that we are the children of the Creator, and as such are Divine, unconquerable and invincible. With this knowledge life is a joy; hardships and experiences can be looked upon as adventures, for we have but to realise our power, to be true to our Divinity, when these melt away like mist in the sunshine. God did indeed give His children dominion over all things.

Our souls will guide us, if we will only listen, in every circumstance, every difficulty; and the mind and body so directed will pass through life radiating happiness and perfect health, as free from all cares and responsibilities as the small trusting child.

CHAPTER III.

Our souls are perfect, being children of the Creator, and everything they tell us to do is for our good.

HEALTH is, therefore, the true realisation of what we are: we are perfect: we are children of God. There is no striving to gain what we have already attained. We are merely here to manifest in material form the perfection with which we have been endowed from the beginning of all time. Health is listening solely to the commands of our souls; in being trustful as little children; in rejecting intellect (that tree of the knowledge of good and evil) with its reasonings, its 'fors' and 'againsts,' its anticipatory fears: ignoring convention, the trivial ideas and commands of other people, so that we can pass through life untouched, unharmed, free to serve our fellow-men.

We can judge our health by our happiness, and by our happiness we can know that we are obeying the dictates of our souls. It is not necessary to be a monk, a nun, or hide away from the world; the world is for us to enjoy and to serve, and it is only by serving out of love and happiness that we can truly be of use, and do our best work. A thing done from a sense of duty with, perhaps, a feeling of irritation and impatience is of no account at all, it is merely precious time wasted when there might be a brother in real need of our help.

Truth has no need to be analysed, argued about, or wrapped up in many words. It is realised in a flash, it is part of you. It is only about the unessential complicated things of life that we need so much convincing, and that have led to the development of the intellect. The things that count are simple, they are the ones that make you say, "why, that is true, I seem to have known that always," and so is the realisation of the happiness that comes to us when we are in harmony with our spiritual self, and the closer the union the more intense the joy. Think of the radiance one sometimes sees in a bride on her wedding morn; the rapture of a mother with a new-born babe; the ecstasy of an artist completing a masterpiece: such are the moments where there is spiritual union.

Think how wonderful life would be if we lived it all in such joy: and so it is possible when we lose ourselves in our life's work.

CHAPTER IV.

If we follow our own instincts, our own wishes, our own thoughts, our own desires, we should never know anything but joy and health.

NEITHER is it a difficult far-away attainment to hear the voice of our own soul; it has all been made so simple for us if we will but acknowledge it. Simplicity is the keynote of all Creation.

Our soul (the still small voice, God's own voice) speaks to us through our intuition, our instincts, through our desires, ideals, our ordinary likes and dislikes; in whichever way it is easiest for us individually to hear. How else can He speak to us? Our true instincts, desires, likes or dislikes are given us so that we can interpret the spiritual commands of our soul by means of our limited physical perceptions, for it is not possible for many of us yet to be in direct communion with our Higher Self. These commands are meant to be followed implicitly, because the soul alone knows what experiences are necessary for that particular personality. Whatever the command may be, trivial or important, the desire for another cup of tea, or a complete change of the whole of one's life's habits, it should be willingly obeyed. The soul knows that satiation is the one real cure for all that we, in this world, consider as sin and wrong, for until the whole being revolts against a certain act, that fault is not eradicated but simply dormant, just as it is much better and quicker to go on sticking one's fingers into the jam-pot until one is so sick that jam has no further attraction.

Our true desires, the wishes of our true selves, are not to be confused with the wishes and desires of other people so often implanted in our minds, or of conscience, which is another word for the same thing. We must pay no heed to the world's interpretation of our actions. Our own soul alone is responsible for our good, our reputation is in His keeping; we can rest assured that there is only one sin, that of not obeying the dictates of our own Divinity. That is the sin against God and our neighbour. These wishes, intuitions, desires are never selfish; they concern ourselves alone and are always right for us, and bring us health in body and mind.

Disease is the result in the physical body of the resistance of the personality to the guidance of the soul. It is when we turn a deaf ear to the 'still small voice,' and forget the Divinity within us; when we try to force our wishes upon others, or allow their suggestions, thoughts, and commands to influence us.

The more we become free from outside influences, from other personalities, the more our soul can use us to do His work.

It is only when we attempt to control and rule someone else that we are selfish. But the world tries to tell us that it is selfishness to follow our own desires. That is because the world wishes to enslave us, for truly it is only when we can realise and be unhampered in our real selves that we can be used for the good of mankind. It is the great truth of Shakespeare, "To thine own self be true, and it must follow, as the night the day, thou canst not then be false to any man."

The bee, by its very choice of a particular flower for its honey, is the means used to bring it the pollen necessary for the future life of its young plants.

CHAPTER V.

It is allowing the interference of other people that stops our listening to the dictates of our soul, and that brings disharmony and disease. The moment the thought of another person enters our minds, it deflects us from our true course.

GOD gave us each our birthright, an individuality of our very own: He gave us each our own particular work to do, which only we can do: He gave us each our own particular path to follow with which nothing must interfere. Let us see to it that not only do we allow no interference, but, and even more important, that we in no way whatsoever interfere with any other single human being. In this lies true health, true service, and the fulfilment of our purpose on earth.

Interferences occur in every life, they are part of the Divine Plan, they are necessary so that we can learn to stand up to them: in fact, we can look upon them as really useful opponents, merely there to help us gain in strength, and realise our Divinity and our invincibility. And we can also know that it is only when we allow them to affect us that they gain in importance and tend to check our progress. It rests entirely with us how quickly we progress: whether we allow interference in our Divine mission; whether we accept the manifestation of interference (called disease) and let it limit and injure our bodies; or whether, we, as children of God, use these to establish us the more firmly in our purpose.

The more the apparent difficulties in our path the more we may be certain that our mission is worth while. Florence Nightingale reached her ideal in the face of a nation's opposition: Galileo believed the world was round in spite of the entire world's disbelief, and the ugly ducking became the swan although his whole family scorned him.

We have no right whatever to interfere with the life of any one of God's children. Each of us has our own job, in the doing of which only we have the power and knowledge to bring it to perfection. It is only when we forget this fact, and try and force our work on others, or let them interfere with ours that friction and disharmony occur in our being.

This disharmony, disease, makes itself manifest in the body, for the body merely serves to reflect the workings of the soul; just as the face reflects happiness by smiles, or temper by frowns. And so in bigger things; the body will reflect the true causes of disease (which are such as fear, indecision, doubt, etc.) in the disarrangement of its systems and tissues.

Disease, therefore, is the result of interference: interfering with someone else or allowing ourselves to be interfered with.

CHAPTER VI.

All we have to do is to preserve our personality, to live our own life, to be captain of our own ship, and all will be well.

THERE are great qualities in which all men are gradually perfecting themselves, possibly concentrating upon one or two at a time. They are those which have been manifested in the earthly lives of all the Great Masters who have, from time to time, come into the world to teach us, and help us to see the easy and simple way of overcoming all our difficulties.

These are such as —

LOVE.
SYMPATHY.
PEACE.
STEADFASTNESS.
GENTLENESS.
STRENGTH.
UNDERSTANDING.
TOLERANCE.
WISDOM.
FORGIVENESS.
COURAGE.
JOY.

And it is by perfecting these qualities in ourselves that each one of us is raising the whole world a step nearer to its final unthinkably glorious goal. We realise then that we are seeking no selfish gain of personal merit, but that every single human being, rich or poor, high or low, is of the same importance in the Divine Plan, and is given the same mighty privilege of being a saviour of the world simply by knowing that he is a perfect child of the Creator.

As there are these qualities, these steps to perfection, so there are hindrances, or interferences which serve to strengthen us in our determination to stand firm.

These are the real causes of disease, and are of such as —

RESTRAINT.
FEAR.
RESTLESSNESS.
INDECISION.
INDIFFERENCE.
WEAKNESS.
DOUBT.
OVER-ENTHUSIASM.
IGNORANCE.
IMPATIENCE.
TERROR.
GRIEF.

These, if we allow them, will reflect themselves in the body causing what we call disease. Not understanding the real causes we have attributed disharmony to external influences, germs, cold, heat, and have given names to the results, arthritis, cancer, asthma, etc.: thinking that disease begins in the physical body.

There are then definite groups of mankind, each group performing its own function, that is, manifesting in the material world the particular lesson he has learnt. Each individual in these groups has a definite personality of his own, a definite work to do, and a definite individual way of doing that work. There are also causes of disharmony, which unless we hold to our definite personality and our work, may react upon the body in the form of disease.

Real health is happiness, and a happiness so easy of attainment because it is a happiness in small things; doing the things that we really love to do, being with the people that we truly like. There is no strain, no effort, no striving for the unattainable, health is there for us to accept any time we like. It is to find out and do the work that we are really suited for. So many suppress their real desires and become square pegs in round holes: through the wishes of a parent a son may become a solicitor, a soldier, a business man, when his true desire is to become a carpenter: or through the ambitions of a mother to see her daughter well married, the world may lose another Florence Nightingale. This sense of duty is then a false sense of duty, and a dis-service to the world; it results in unhappiness and, probably, the greater part of a lifetime wasted before the mistake can be rectified.

There was a Master once Who said, "Know ye not that I must be about My Father's business?" meaning that He must obey His Divinity and not His earthly parents.

Let us find the one thing in life that attracts us most and do it. Let that one thing be so part of us that it is as natural as breathing; as natural as it is for the bee to collect honey, and the tree to shed its old leaves in the autumn and bring forth new ones in the spring. If we study nature we find that every creature, bird, tree and flower has its definite part to play, its own definite and peculiar work through which it aids and enriches the entire Universe. The very worm, going about its daily job, helps to drain and purify the earth: the earth provides for the nutriment of all green things; and, in turn, vegetation sustains mankind and every living creature, returning in due course to enrich the soil. Their life is one of beauty and usefulness, their work is so natural to them that it is their life.

And our own work, when we find it, so belongs to us, so fits us, that it is effortless, it is easy, it is a joy: we never tire of it, it is our hobby. It brings out in us our true personality, all the talents and capabilities waiting within each one of us to be manifested: in it we are happy and at home; and it is only when we are happy (which is obeying the commands of our soul) that we can do our best work.

We may have already found our right work, then what fun life is! Some from childhood have the knowledge of what they are meant to do, and keep to it throughout their lives: and some know in childhood, but are deterred by contra-suggestions and circumstances, and the discouragement of others. Yet we can all get back to our ideals, and even though we cannot realise them immediately we can go on seeking to do so, then the very seeking will bring us comfort, for our souls are very patient with us. The right desire, the right motive, no matter what the result, is the thing that counts, the real success.

So if you would rather be a farmer than a lawyer; if you would rather be a barber than a bus-driver, or a cook than a greengrocer, change your occupation, be what you want to be: and then you will be happy and well, then you will work with zest, and then you will be doing finer work as a farmer, a barber, a cook, than you could ever achieve in the occupation that never belonged to you.

And then you will be obeying the dictates of your Spiritual Self.

CHAPTER VII.

Once we realise our own Divinity the rest is easy.

IN the beginning God gave man dominion over all things. Man, the child of the Creator, has a deeper reason for his disharmony than the draught from an open window. Our 'fault lies not in our stars, but in ourselves,' and how full of gratitude and hope can we be when we realise that the cure also lies within ourselves! Remove the disharmony, the fear, the terror, or the indecision, and we regain harmony between soul and mind, and the body is once more perfect in all its parts.

Whatever the disease, the result of this disharmony, we may be quite sure that the cure is well within our powers of accomplishment, for our souls never ask of us more than we can very easily do.

Everyone of us is a healer, because every one of us at heart has a love for something, for our fellow-men, for animals, for nature, for beauty in some form, and we every one of us wish to protect and help it to increase. Everyone of us also has sympathy with those in distress, and naturally so, because we have all been in distress ourselves at some time in our lives. So that not only can we heal ourselves, but we have the great privilege of being able to help others to heal themselves, and the only qualifications necessary are love and sympathy.

We, as children of the Creator, have within us all perfection, and we come into this world merely that we may realise our Divinity; so that all tests and all experiences will leave us untouched, for through that Divine Power all things are possible to us.

CHAPTER VIII.

The healing herbs are those which have been given the power to help us preserve our personality.

JUST as God in His mercy has given us food to eat, so has He placed amongst the herbs of the fields beautiful plants to heal us when we are sick. These are there to extend a helping hand to man in those dark hours of forgetfulness when he loses sight of his Divinity, and allows the cloud of fear or pain to obscure his vision.

Such herbs are —

Chicory	*(Cichorium intybus)*
Mimulus	*(Mimulus luteus)*
Agrimony	*(Agrimonia eupatoria)*
Scleranthus	*(Scleranthus annuus)*
Clematis	*(Clematis vitalba)*
Centaury	*(Erythraea centaurium)*
Gentian	*(Gentiana amarella)*
Vervain	*(Verbena officinalis)*
Cerato	*(Ceratostigma willmottiana)*
Impatiens	*(Impatiens royalei)*
Rock Rose	*(Helianthemum vulgare)*
Water Violet	*(Hottonia palustris)*

Each herb corresponds with one of the qualities, and its purpose is to strengthen that quality so that the personality may rise above the fault that is the particular stumbling block.

The following table will indicate the quality, the fault, and the remedy which aids the personality to dispel that fault.

Failing.		*Herb.*		*Virtue.*
Restraint	......	Chicory	......	Love
Fear	......	Mimulus	......	Sympathy
Restlessness	......	Agrimony	......	Peace

Indecision	......	Scleranthus	......	Steadfastness
Indifference	......	Clematis	......	Gentleness
Weakness	......	Centaury	......	Strength
Doubt	....	Gentian	......	Understanding
Over-enthusiasm	......	Vervain	......	Tolerance
Ignorance	......	Cerato	......	Wisdom
Impatience	......	Impatiens	......	Forgiveness
Terror	....	Rock Rose	......	Courage
Grief	....	Water Violet	......	Joy

The remedies are endowed with a definite healing power quite apart from faith, neither does their action depend upon the one who administers them, just as a sedative sends a patient to sleep whether given by the nurse or the doctor.

CHAPTER IX.

The real nature of disease.

IN true healing the nature and the name of the physical disease is of no consequence whatever. Disease of the body itself is nothing but the result of the disharmony between soul and mind. It is only a symptom of the cause, and as the same cause will manifest itself differently in nearly every individual, seek to remove this cause, and the after results, whatever they may be, will disappear automatically.

We can understand this more clearly by taking as an example the suicide. All suicides do not drown themselves. Some throw themselves from a height, some take poison, but behind it all is despair: help them to overcome their despair and find someone or something to live for, and they are cured permanently: simply taking away the poison will only save them for the time being, they may later make another attempt. Fear also reacts upon people in quite different ways: some will turn pale, some will flush, some become hysterical and some speechless. Explain the fear to them, show them that they are big enough to overcome and face anything, then nothing can frighten them again. The child will not mind the shadows on the wall if he is given the candle and shown how to make them dance up and down.

We have so long blamed the germ, the weather, the food we eat as the causes of disease; but many of us are immune in an influenza epidemic; many love the exhilaration of a cold wind, and many can eat cheese and drink black coffee late at night with no ill effects. Nothing in nature can hurt us when we are happy and in harmony, on the contrary all nature is there for our use and our enjoyment. It is only when we allow doubt and depression, indecision or fear to creep in that we are sensitive to outside influences.

It is, therefore, the real cause behind the disease, which is of the utmost importance; the mental state of the patient himself, not the condition of his body.

Any disease, however serious, however long-standing, will be cured by restoring to the patient happiness, and desire to carry on with his work in life. Very often it is only some slight alteration in his mode of life, some little fixed idea that is making him intolerant of others, some mistaken sense of responsibility that keeps him in slavery when he might be doing such good work.

There are seven beautiful stages in the healing of disease, these are —

> PEACE.
> HOPE.
> JOY.
> FAITH.
> CERTAINTY.
> WISDOM.
> LOVE.

CHAPTER X.

To gain freedom, give freedom.

THE ultimate goal of all mankind is perfection, and to gain this state man must learn to pass through all experiences unaffected; he must encounter all interferences and temptations without being deflected from his course: then he is free of all life's difficulties, hardships and sufferings: he has stored up in his soul the perfect love, wisdom, courage, tolerance and understanding that is the result of knowing and seeing everything, for the perfect master is he who has been through every branch of his trade.

We can make this journey a short joyful adventure if we realise that freedom from bondage is only gained by giving freedom; we are set free if we set others free, for it is only by example we can teach. When we have given freedom to every human being with whom we are in contact; when we have given freedom to every creature, everything around us, then we are free ourselves: when we see that we do not, even in the minutest detail, attempt to dominate, control, or influence the life of another, we shall find that interference has passed out of our own lives, because it is those that we bind who bind us. There was a certain young man who was so bound to his possessions that he could not accept a Divine gift.

And we can free ourselves from the domination of others so easily, firstly by giving them absolute freedom, and secondly, by very gently, very lovingly, refusing to be dominated by them. Lord Nelson was very wise in placing his blind eye to the telescope on one occasion. No force, no resentment, no hatred, and no unkindness is necessary. Our opponents are our friends, they make the game worth while, and we shall all shake hands at the end of the match.

We must not expect others to do what we want, their ideas are the right ideas for them, and though their pathway may lead in a different direction from ours, the goal at the end of the journey is the same for us all. We do find that it is when we want others to 'fall in with our wishes' that we fall out with them.

We are like cargo-ships bound for the different countries of the world, some for Africa, some for Canada, some for Australia, then returning to the same home port. Why follow another ship to Canada when our destination is Australia? It means such a delay.

Again, we perhaps do not realise what small things may bind us, the very things that we wish to hold are the things that are holding us: it may be a house, a garden, a piece of furniture; even they have their right to freedom. Worldly possessions, after all are transient, they give rise to anxiety and worry because inwardly we know of their inevitable and ultimate loss. They are there to be enjoyed and admired and used to their full capacity, but not to gain so much importance that they become chains to bind us.

If we set everybody and everything around us at liberty, we find that in return we are richer in love and possessions than ever we were before, for the love that gives freedom is the great love that binds the closer.

CHAPTER XI.

Healing.

FROM time immemorial humanity has recognised that our Creator in His love for us has placed herbs in the fields for our healing, just as He has provided the corn and the fruit for our sustenance.

Astrologers, those who have studied the stars, and herbalists, those who have studied the plants, have ever been seeking those remedies which will help us to keep our health and joy.

To find the herb that will help us we must find the object of our life, what we are striving to do, and also understand the difficulties in our path. The difficulties we call faults or failings, but let us not mind these faults and failings, because they are the very proof to us that we are attaining bigger things: our faults should be our encouragements, because they mean that we are aiming high. Let us find for ourselves which of the battles we are particularly fighting, which adversary we are especially trying to overcome, and then take with gratitude and thankfulness that plant which has been sent to help us to victory. We should accept these beautiful herbs of the fields as a sacrament, as our Creator's Divine gift to aid us in our troubles.

In true healing there is no thought whatever of the disease: it is the mental state, the mental difficulty alone, to be considered: it is where we are going wrong in the Divine Plan that matters. This disharmony with our Spiritual Self may produce a hundred different failings in our bodies (for our bodies after all merely reproduce the condition of our minds), but what matters that? If we put our mind right the body will soon be healed. It is as Christ said to us, ''Is it easier to say, thy sins be forgiven thee or take up thy bed and walk?''

So again let us clearly understand that our physical illness is of no consequence whatsoever: it is the state of our minds, and that, and that alone, which is of importance. Therefore, ignoring entirely the illness from which we are suffering, we need consider only to which of the following types we belong.

Should any difficulty be found in selecting your own remedy, it will help to ask yourself which of the virtues you most admire in other people; or which of the failings is, in others, your pet aversion, for any fault of which we may still have left a trace and are especially attempting to eradicate, that is the one we most hate to see in other people. It is the way we are encouraged to wipe it out in ourselves.

We are all healers, and with love and sympathy in our natures we are also able to help anyone who really desires health. Seek for the outstanding mental conflict in the patient, give him the remedy that will assist him to overcome that particular fault, and all the encouragement and hope you can, then the healing virtue within him will of itself do all the rest.

Photographs

Dr. Bach rowing, one of his favourite forms of relaxation.
(Courtesy Bach Centre) date unknown

Edward Bach as a young man, circa 1905.
(Courtesy Bach Centre)

Edward Bach, circa 1922.
(Courtesy E. Varney)

Victor Bullen
(1887-1975)

"Victor Bullen, friend and partner of Dr. Bach, for over 40 years had dedicated his life to bringing back happiness and health to a great number of people, not only with the Bach Flower Remedies but by his own happiness, kindness, and understanding. Dr. Bach called him 'the soul of honour and integrity' and trusted him to carry on his work in all its simplicity after his own death. This Victor did most faithfully."

Nora Weeks, 1975

(Courtesy Bach Centre)
c.1950

Nora Gray Weeks
(1896-1978)

Nora Gray Weeks witnessed the whole spectrum of Dr. Bach's discoveries first hand — proving herself to be not only his right hand helper, but someone he could rely on to nurture him during the great development of his increasing sensitivity through the latter 4 years of his life. Her dedication and loving respect for the doctor must be recorded as perhaps the back-bone of his endeavour, for without her supportive resilience it can safely be assumed that the doctor's work might have faltered before completion — for he did indeed suffer greatly, both mentally and physically as an integral part of his great discovery. The doctor bequeathed to her the whole responsibility of his work. For over 40 years Nora, with the help of Victor, continued steadfastly to offer the Bach remedies to the world honouring the simplicity and purity of Dr. Bach's vision.

(Courtesy Bach Centre)
c.1923

c.1920

Dr. Edward Bach with his daughter Bobbie
(Courtesy E. Varney)

c.1917

c.1919

The Authentic
Bach Flower Remedies

Because of the extensive use and popularity of the Bach Flower Remedies and Rescue Remedy, similar products have begun to appear on the market. The following will help you to distinguish the authentic Bach remedies and Rescue Remedy from other products and clear up some of the misconceptions surrounding the differences.

The name **Rescue Remedy** is a federally registered trademark, as is **Bach Flower Remedies**, with the latter applying to 38 specific preparations and the unique philosophy and system of their use. All 38 of the Bach Flower Remedies are officially recognized as over-the-counter homoeopathic medicines and are listed as such in the *Supplement to the Eighth Edition of the Homoeopathic Pharmacopeia of the United States.*

The Bach Flower Remedies and Rescue Remedy are prepared at only one location in the world, the Bach Centre in England, where to this day the same wildflower locations originally discovered by Dr. Bach are still used. Similar products prepared anywhere else in the world that claim to be Bach Flower Remedies or Rescue Remedy are not, nor are they proven to be, Bach remedy 'equivalents.'

Some of these newly released products are not made from real flowers at all, but are prepared by radionic methods or other devices said to duplicate or enhance the 'vibration' of real flowers. Some of these other products are made from real flowers, but not from the species used for the actual Bach Flower Remedies.

In addition, there are products on the market that are actually unauthorized dilutions of the authentic Bach remedies and Rescue Remedy. Unfortunately, some of the literature and occasionally the labeling of these products makes reference to Dr. Bach's name. This tends to create the false impression that they are genuine Bach remedies or Rescue Remedy. They are not.

All authentic Bach Flower Remedies, including Rescue Remedy liquid, come bottled in concentrated liquid form. Rescue Remedy also comes in cream form. These officially recognized preparations all meet stringent FDA and homoeopathic labeling and quality-control laws. Unauthorized dilutions (even by retail stores) of the Bach Remedies or Rescue remedy, resold over the counter, often do not meet these stringent requirements. Furthermore, though appearing smaller in size, one ten-milliliter (one-third ounce) bottle of Bach remedy concentrate may produce as many as seventy bottles of these watered-down products. Additionally, these products have a limited shelf life, and cost the end consumer substantially more money than if they purchased the authentic Bach remedy concentrate directly.

Ultimately, what distinguishes the real Bach Flower Remedies, including Rescue Remedy, from similar products is more than just the name *Bach*. The Bach Flower Remedies and Rescue Remedy have been used worldwide for over fifty years and have consistently proven themselves safe, gentle, and effective by countless numbers of physicians, health care professionals, and the general public. To make sure you are getting the genuine Bach Flower Remedies or Rescue Remedy, look for the manufacturer's name, the **Bach Centre**, England, appearing on the front or side of every label.

The freedom and right to choose are important to us all; equally important is the information and knowledge needed to choose wisely.

Where to Obtain Rescue Remedy and the Other Bach Flower Remedies

In England, and to inquire about distributors in other parts of the world write:

DR. EDWARD BACH CENTRE
Mount Vernon
Sotwell, Wallingford
Oxon., OX10 0PZ, England

This was the home and workplace of Dr. Edward Bach during the latter years. Today, the Dr. Edward Bach Centre still carries on Dr. Bach's work of helping those in need, manufacturing and distributing the Bach Flower Remedies used around the world. Additionally, individual booklets such as Dr. Bach's *The Twelve Healers* and *Heal Thyself*, as well as other materials related to the work may be obtained here.

In North and South America and Japan write:

ELLON (BACH USA)
P.O. Box 320
Woodmere, New York 11598, U.S.A.
516-593-2206

In Germany, Austria, and Switzerland write:

THE GERMAN OFFICE
OF THE BACH CENTRE ENGLAND
c/o M. Scheffer
Eppendorfer Landstr. 32
2000 Hamburg 20
West Germany

Further and Recommended Reading

NOTE: Copies of the books listed below may be ordered in their individual (pamphlet) form, published by C.W. Daniel. These as well as additional information on where to locate Dr. Bach's books in other languages may be obtained from: **The Bach Centre**, Mount Vernon, Sotwell, Wallingford, Oxon., OX10 0PZ, England.

In North and South America including Japan, copies of the above books in English may be obtained from: **Ellon (Bach USA)**, P.O. Box 320, Woodmere, New York 11598, U.S.A.

1. *The Bach Flower Remedies* (three volumes in one) includes *Heal Thyself* by Dr. Edward Bach, *The Twelve Healers and Other Remedies* by Dr. Edward Bach, and *The Bach Remedies Repertory* by Dr. F.J. Wheeler (New Canaan, Connecticut: Keats, 1977). All three volumes originally published by C.W. Daniel, Saffron Walden, Essex, 1931, 1933, and 1952, respectively. [1]

2. *The Medical Discoveries of Edward Bach, Physician* by Nora Weeks (New Canaan, Connecticut: Keats, 1979). Originally published by C.W. Daniel, Saffron Walden, Essex, 1940.

3. *The Handbook of the Bach Flower Remedies* by Philip M. Chancellor (New Canaan, Connecticut: Keats, 1980). Originally published by C.W. Daniel, Saffron Walden, Essex, 1971.

4. *The Guide to the Bach Flower Remedies* by Julian Barnard (C.W. Daniel, Saffron Walden, Essex, 1979).

5. *Introduction to the Benefits of the Bach Flower Remedies* by Jane Evans (C.W. Daniel, Saffron Walden, Essex, 1974).

6. *Dictionary of the Bach Flower Remedies* by T. H. Jones (Surrey, England: Published by author, 1976).

---

1. These separate books as well as all the above are available through the Bach Centre, England.

Contributors Index

Index

Index

ABOUT THE AUTHOR

Over the years, Gregory Vlamis has written numerous articles and organized educational seminars in the field of awareness and natural healing. A tireless worker, he has devoted much of his personal time to assisting non-profit organizations to accomplish their various projects and goals.

In addition to writing *Flowers to the Rescue: The Healing Vision of Dr. Edward Bach*, Mr. Vlamis spent two years researching throughout the United Kingdom. He interviewed those who knew Dr. Bach and uncovered rare letters, photographs, and other biographical material previously unavailable.